FIFTY DOORS OF

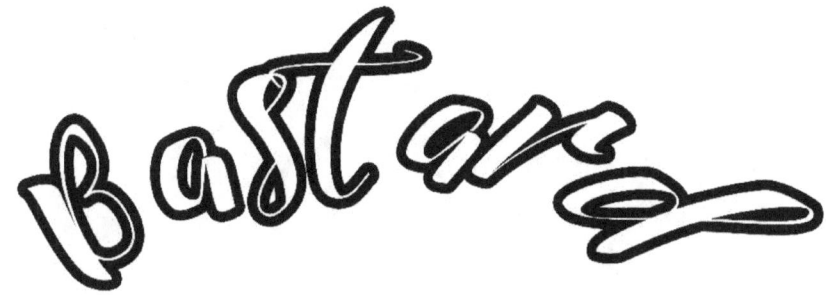

Bastard

40 Swear Words to Color

For Stress Releasing

BY
J.A. FLORENTINE

Happy Coloring!

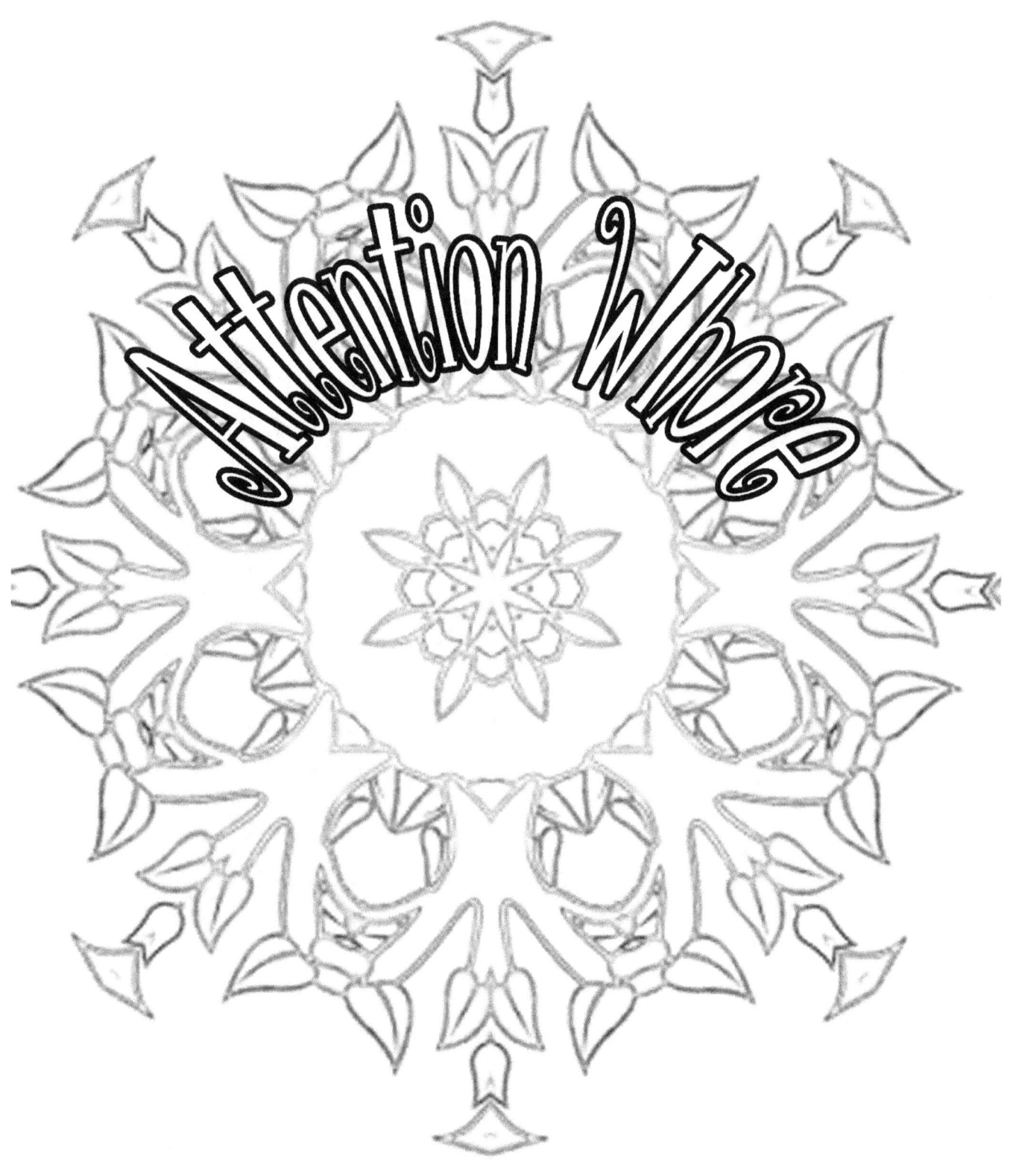

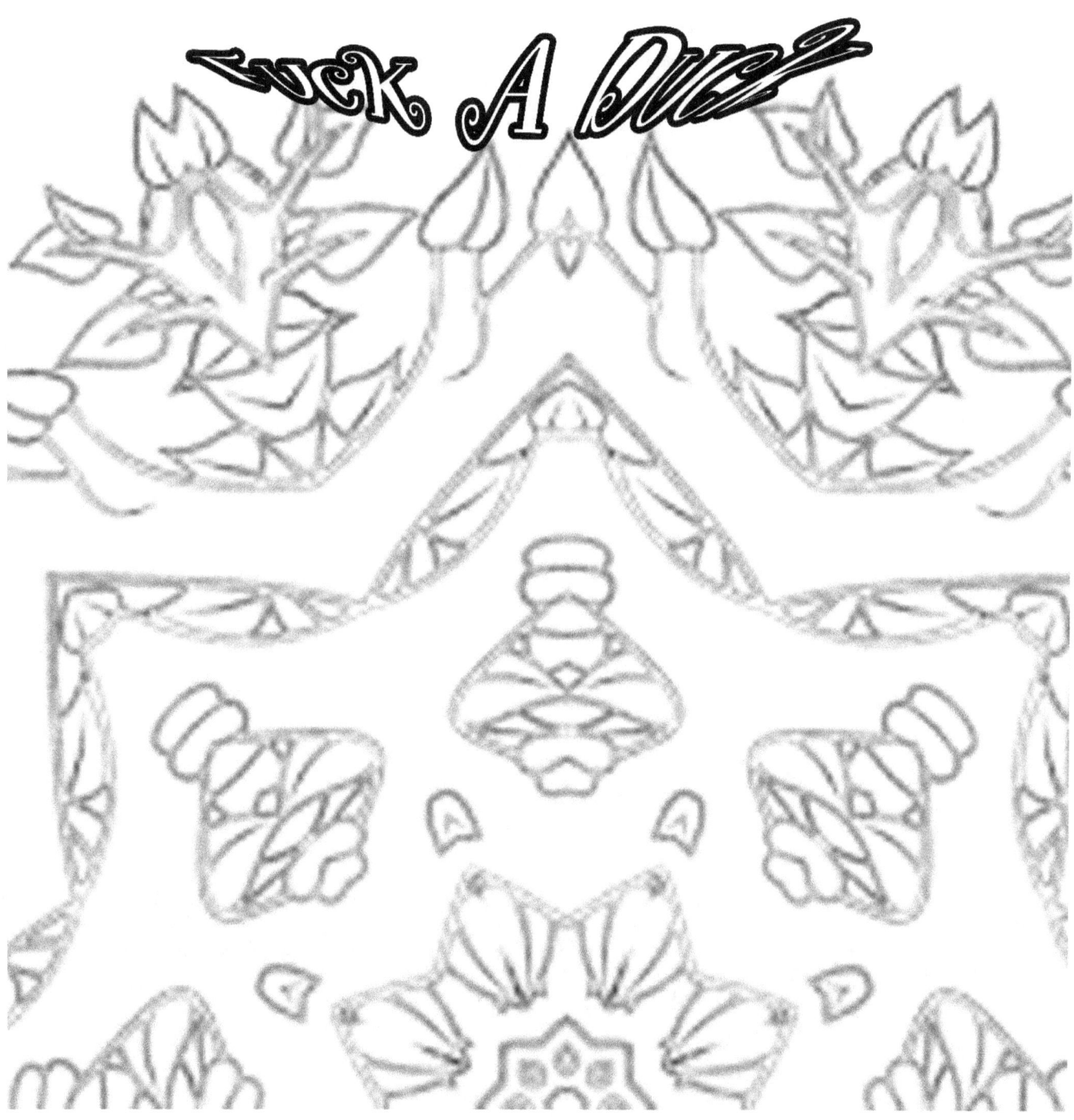

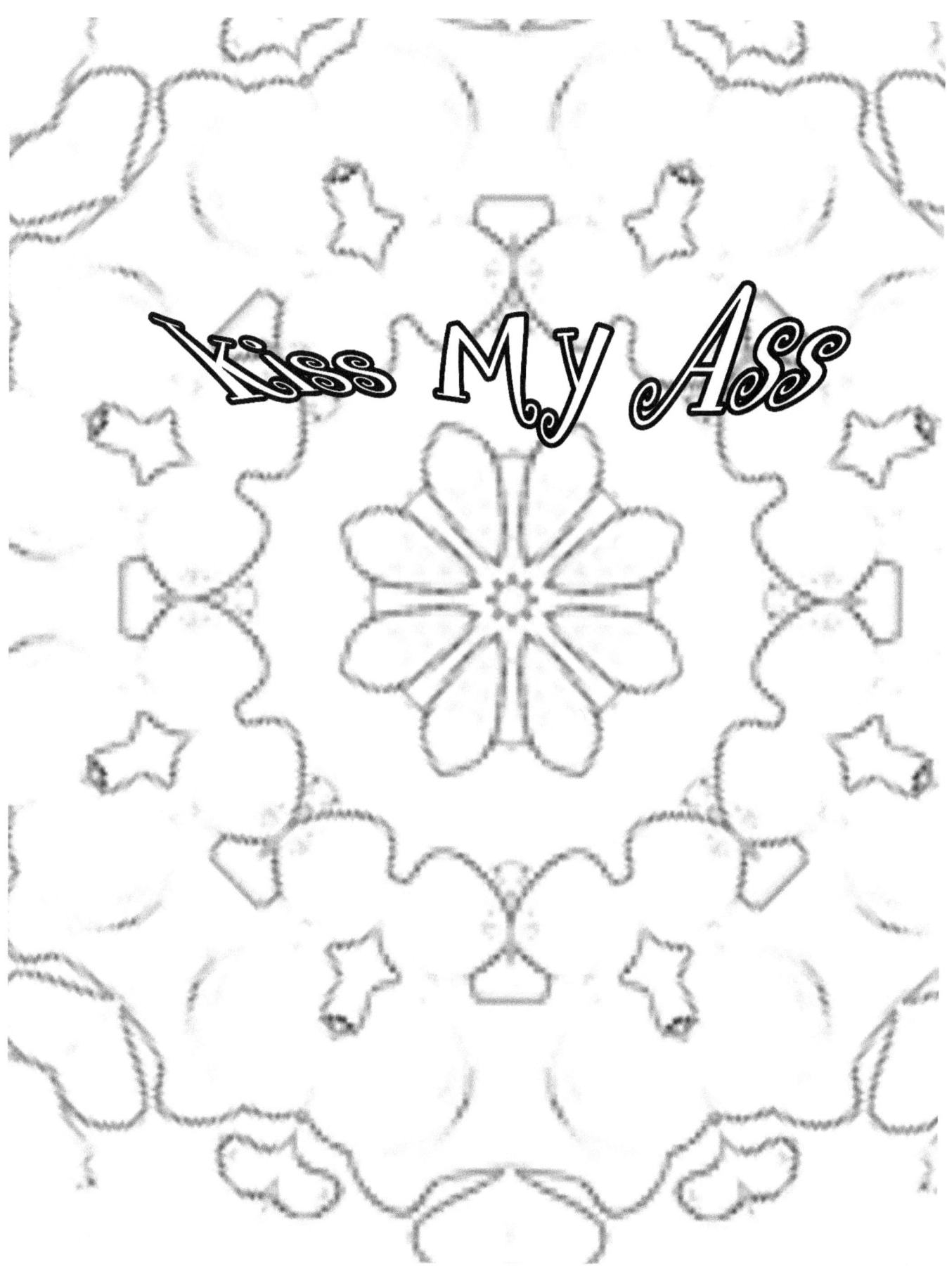

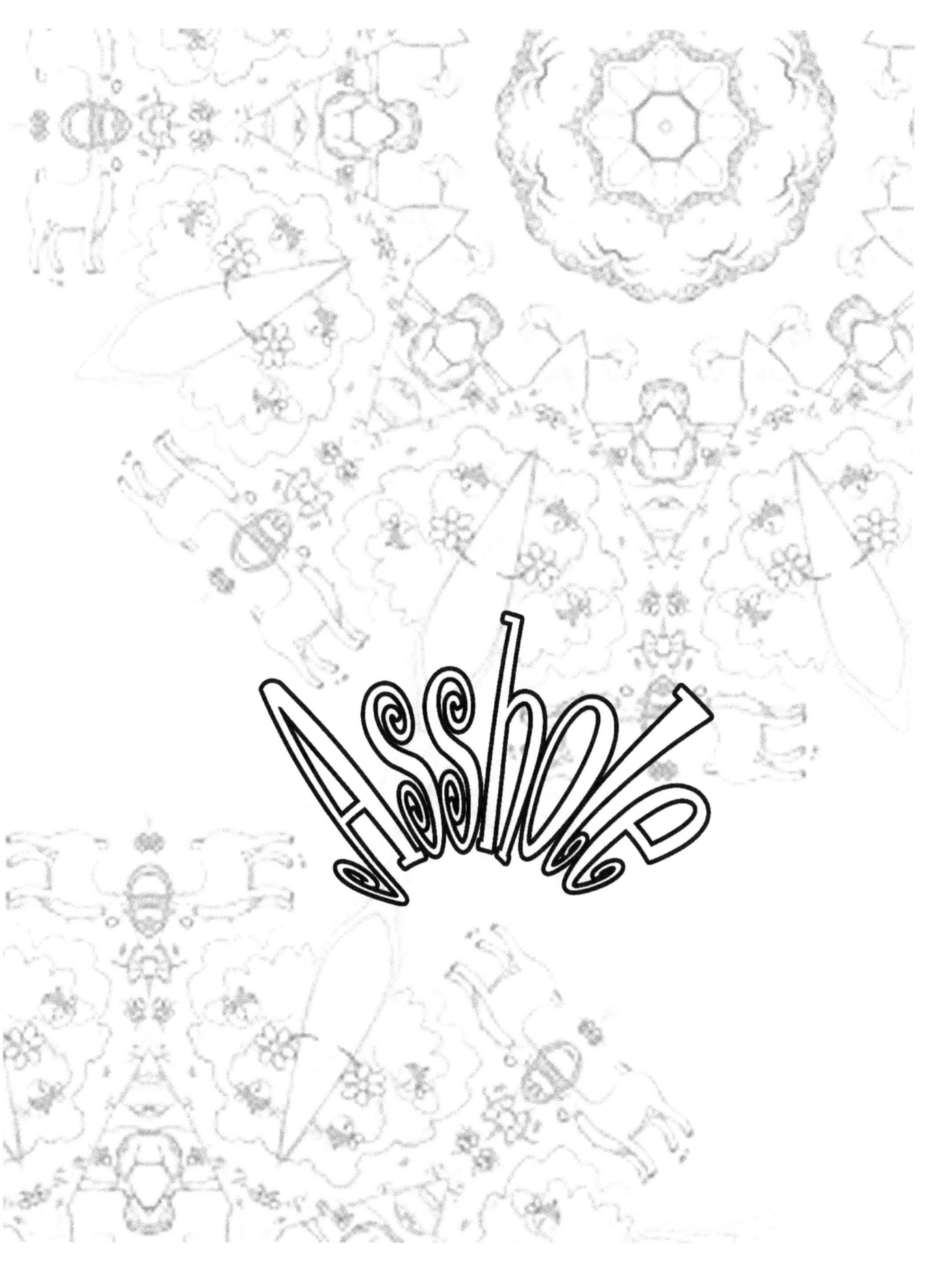

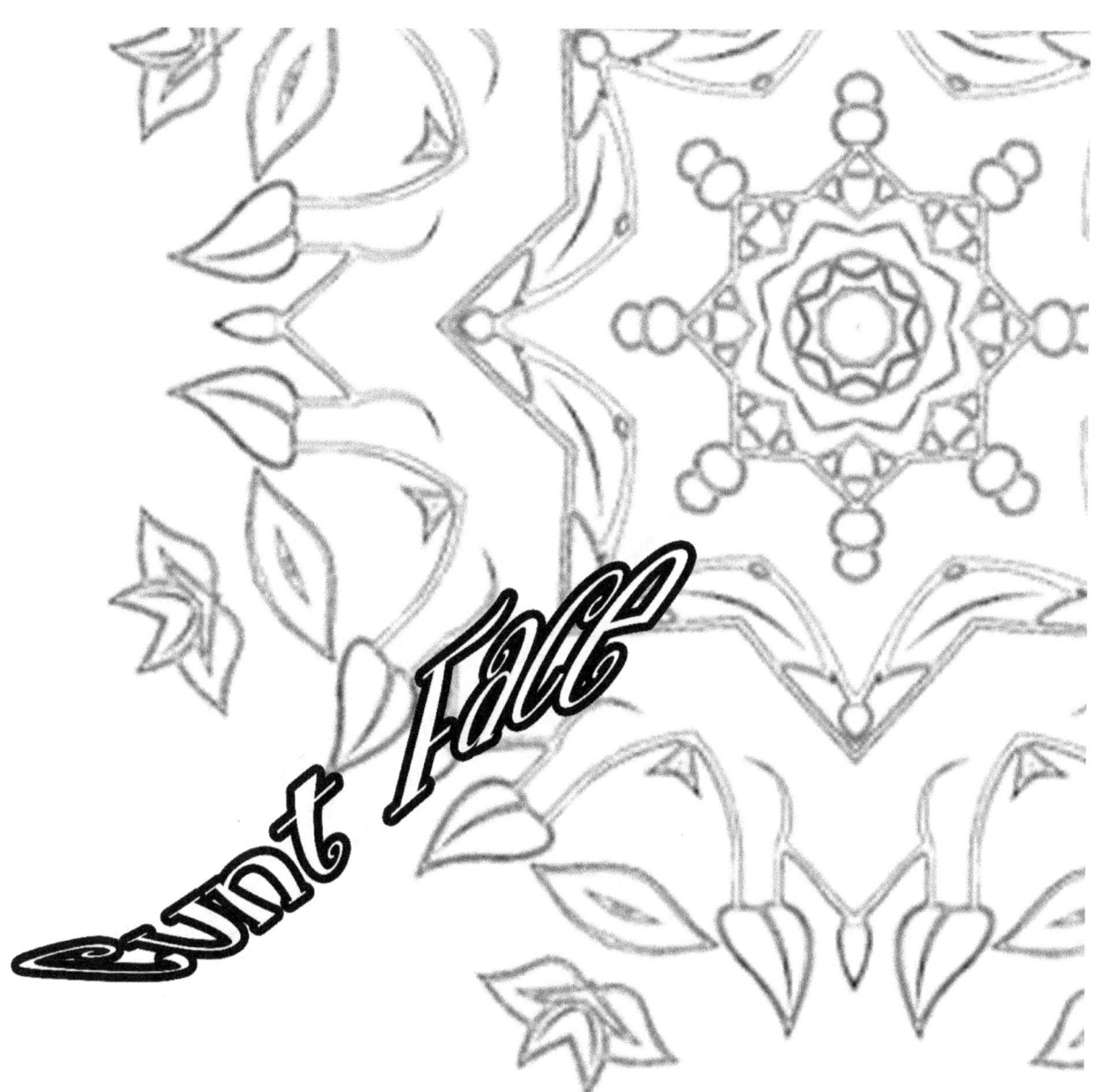

Cock and Balls

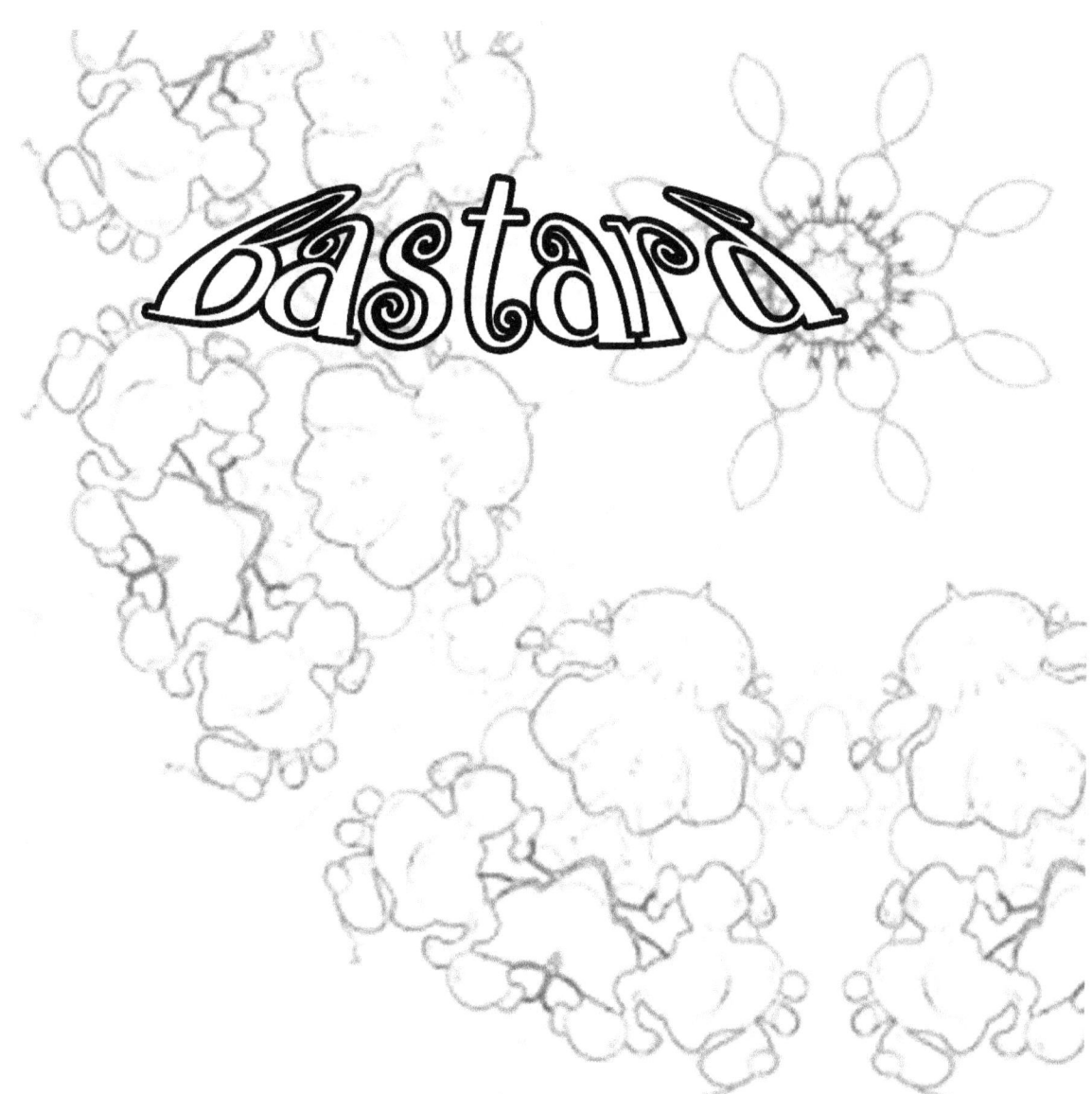

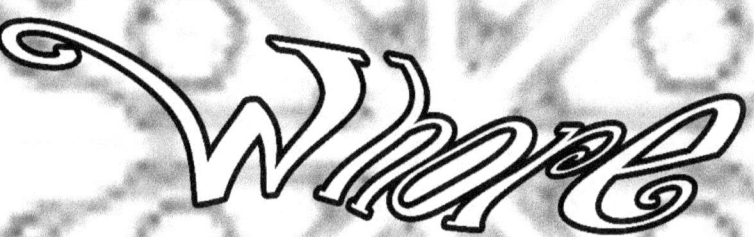

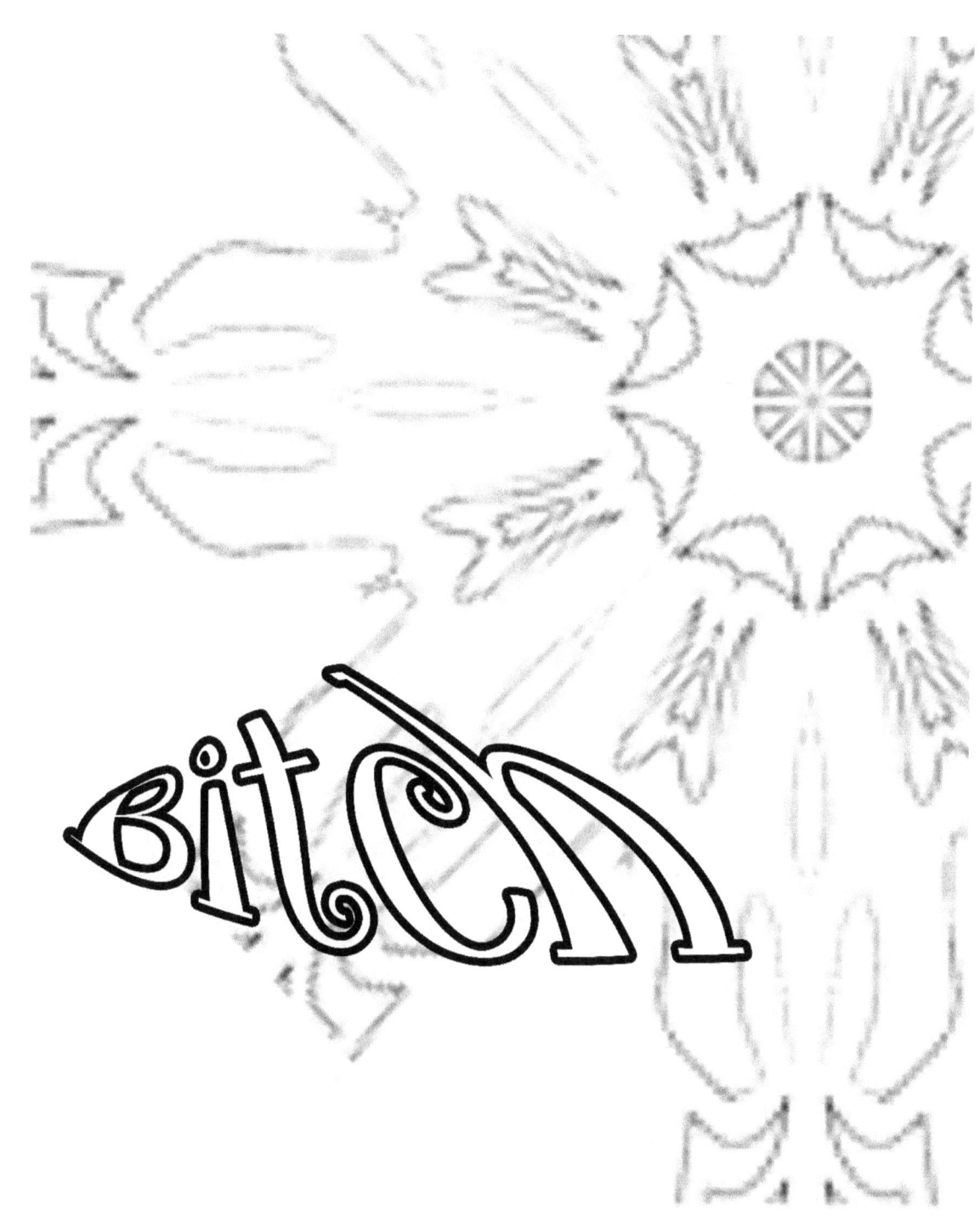

Bullshit

Low Life

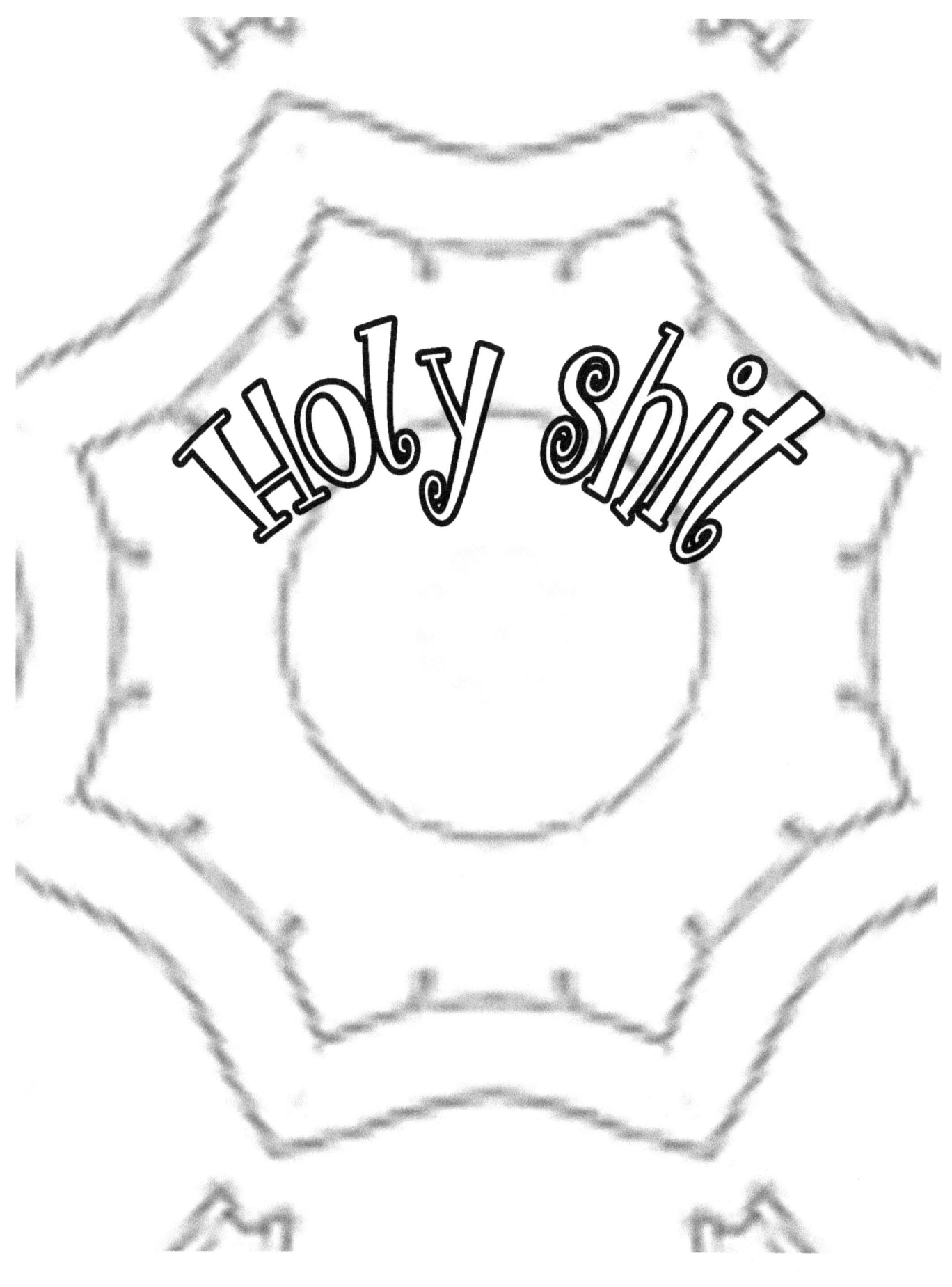

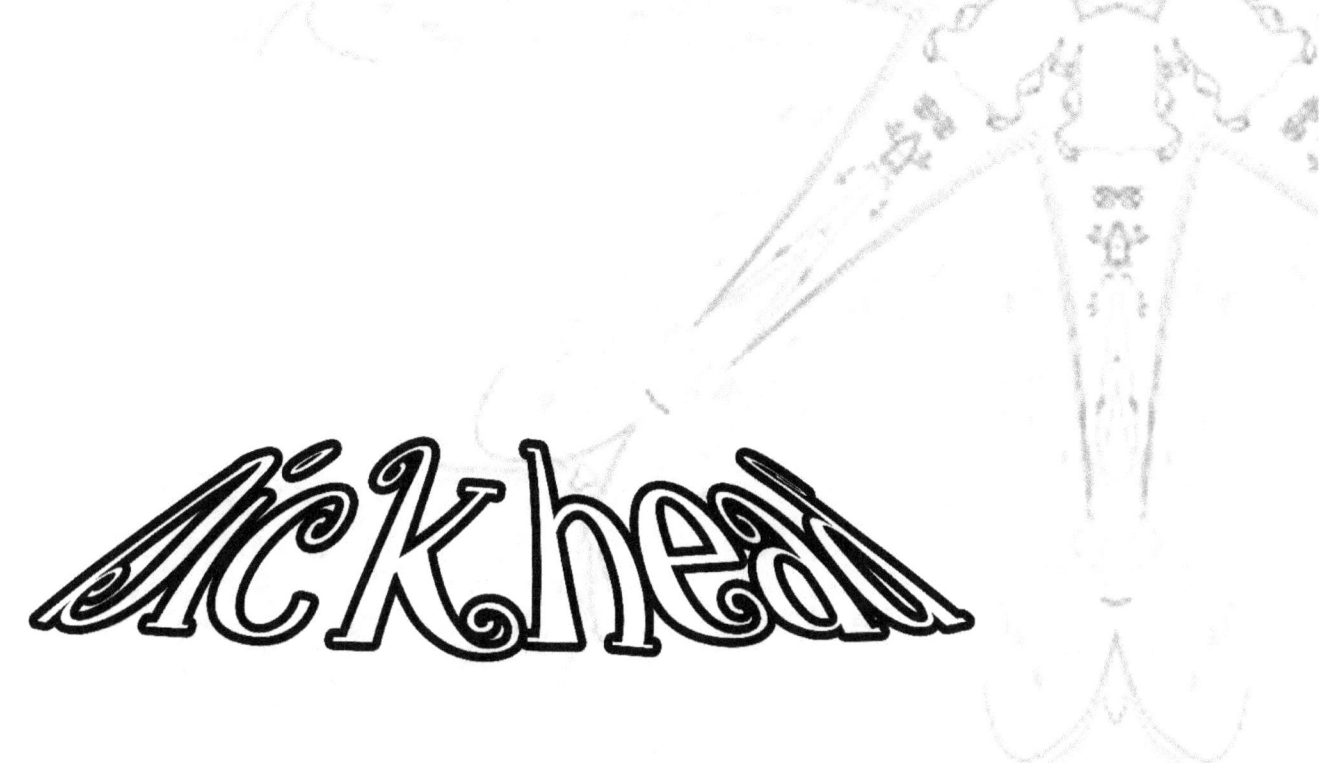

lickhead

Ugly Big shoes

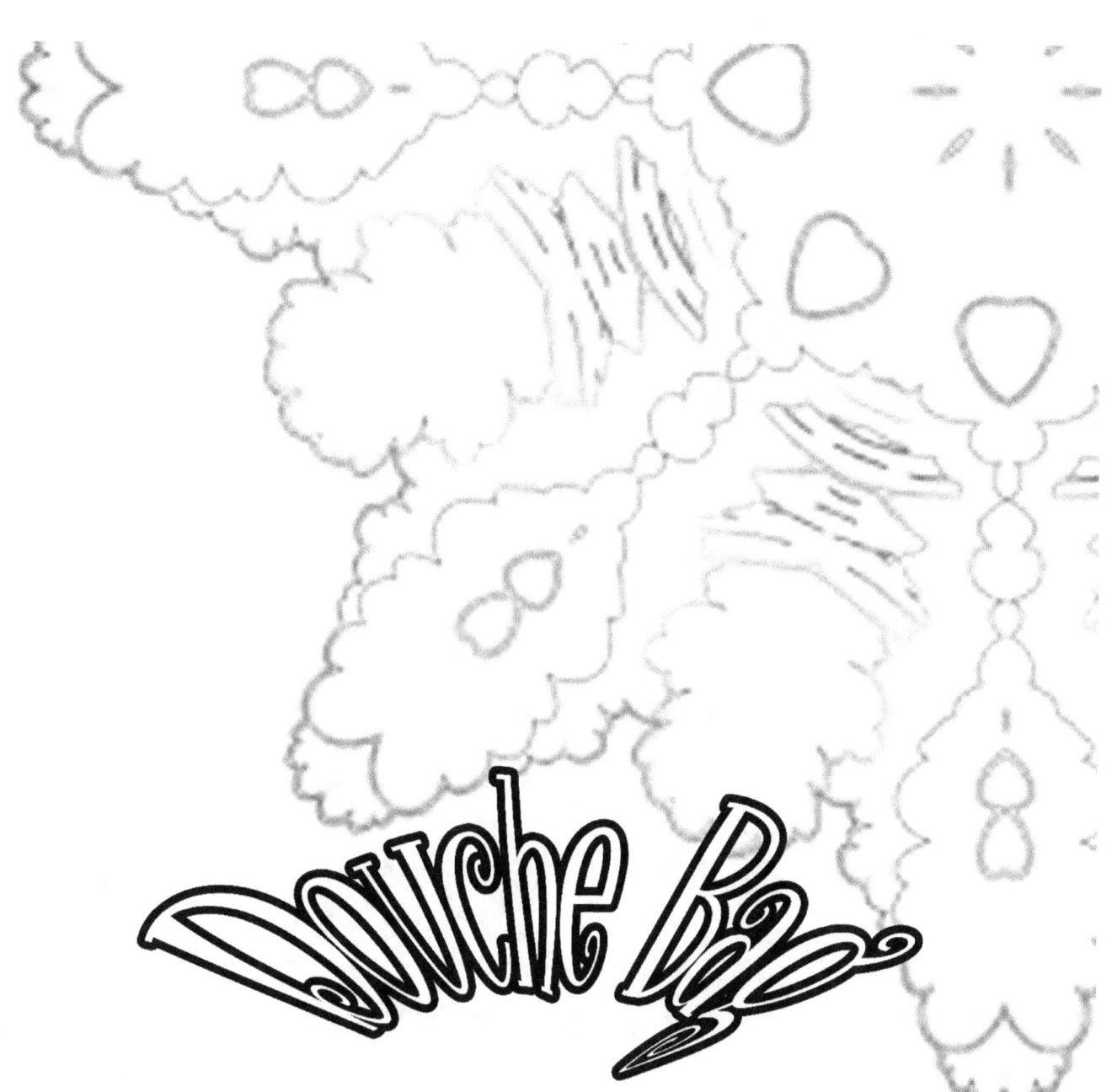

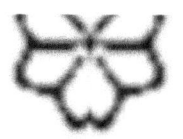

Dick Midget

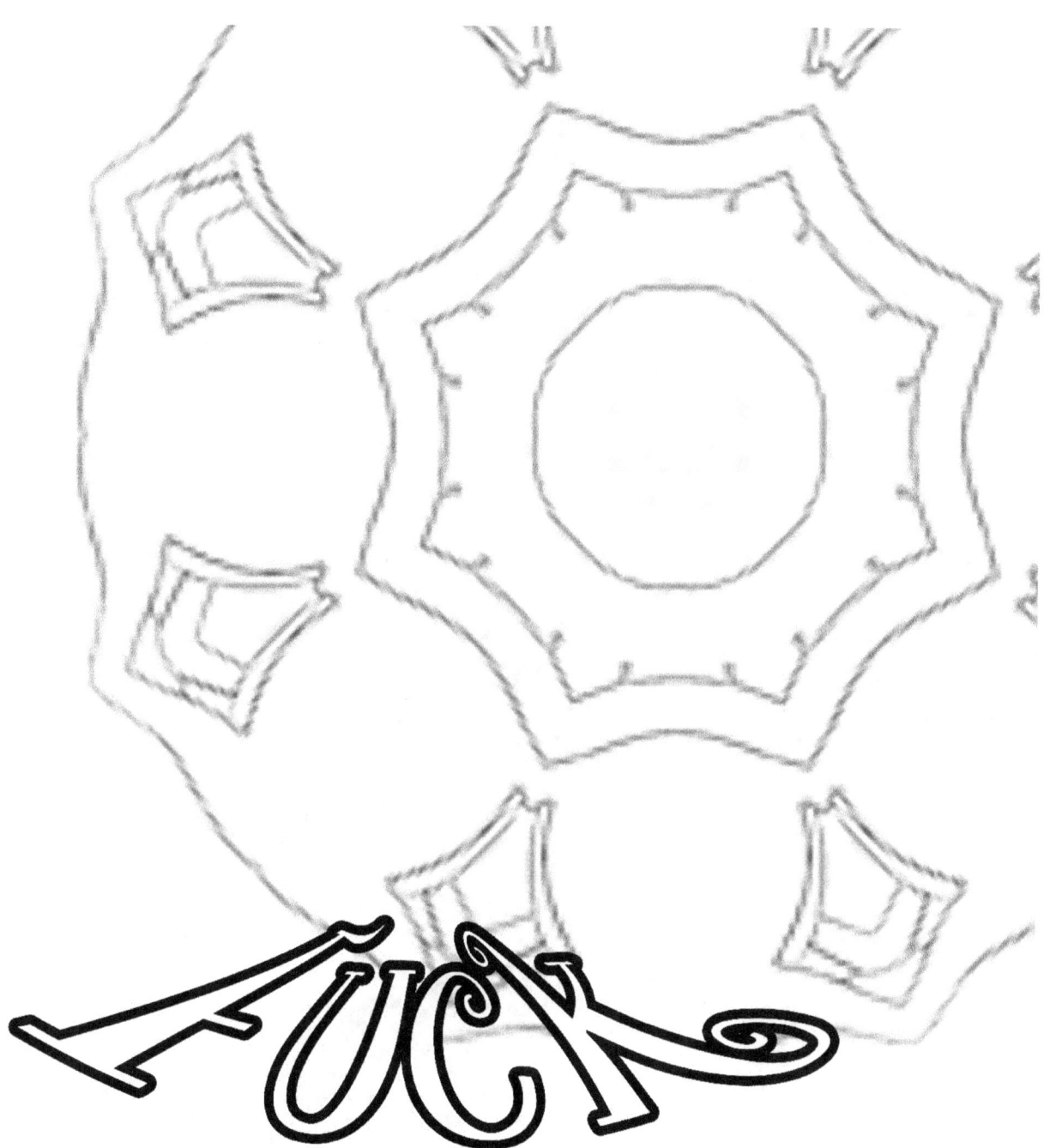

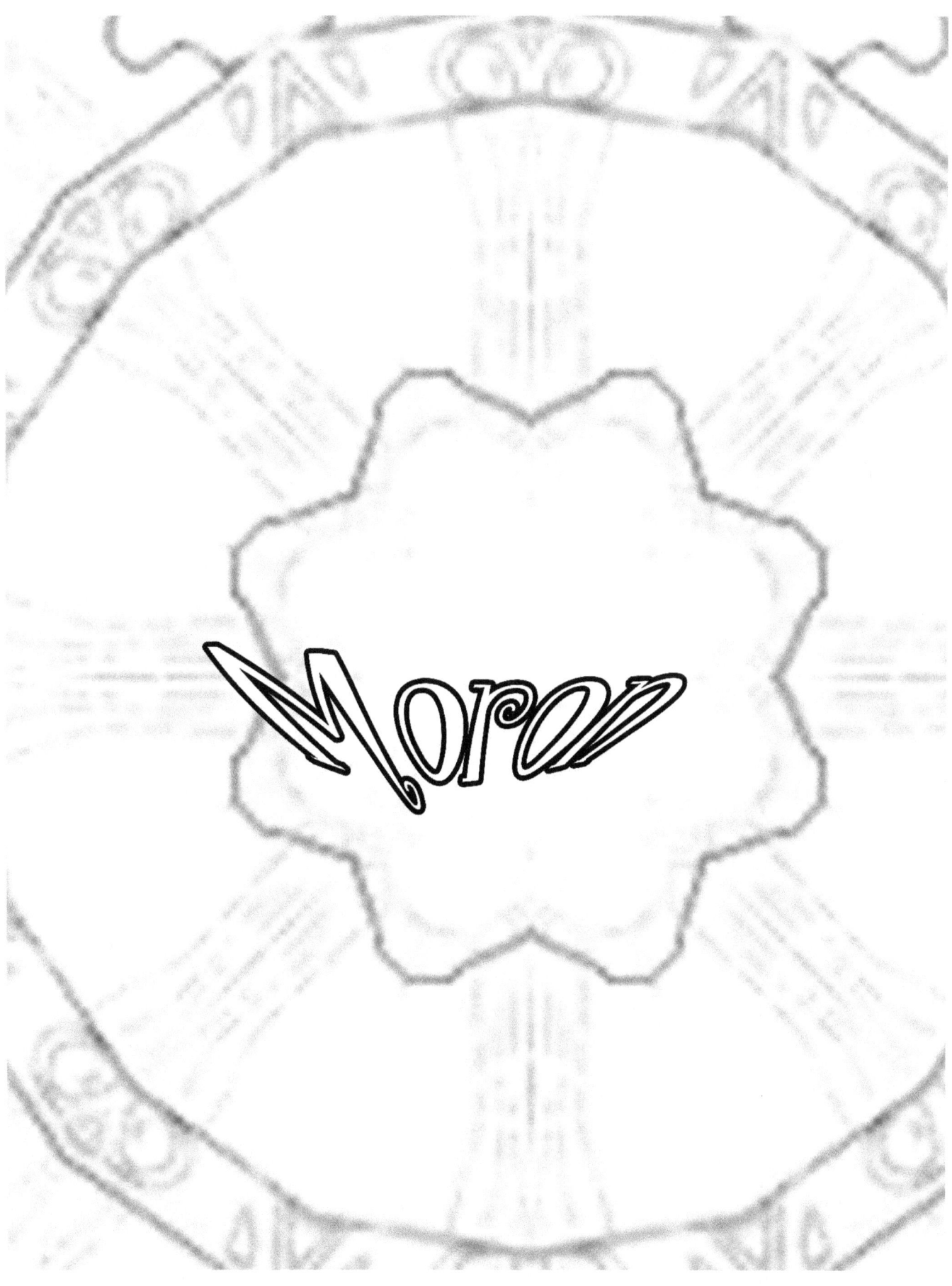

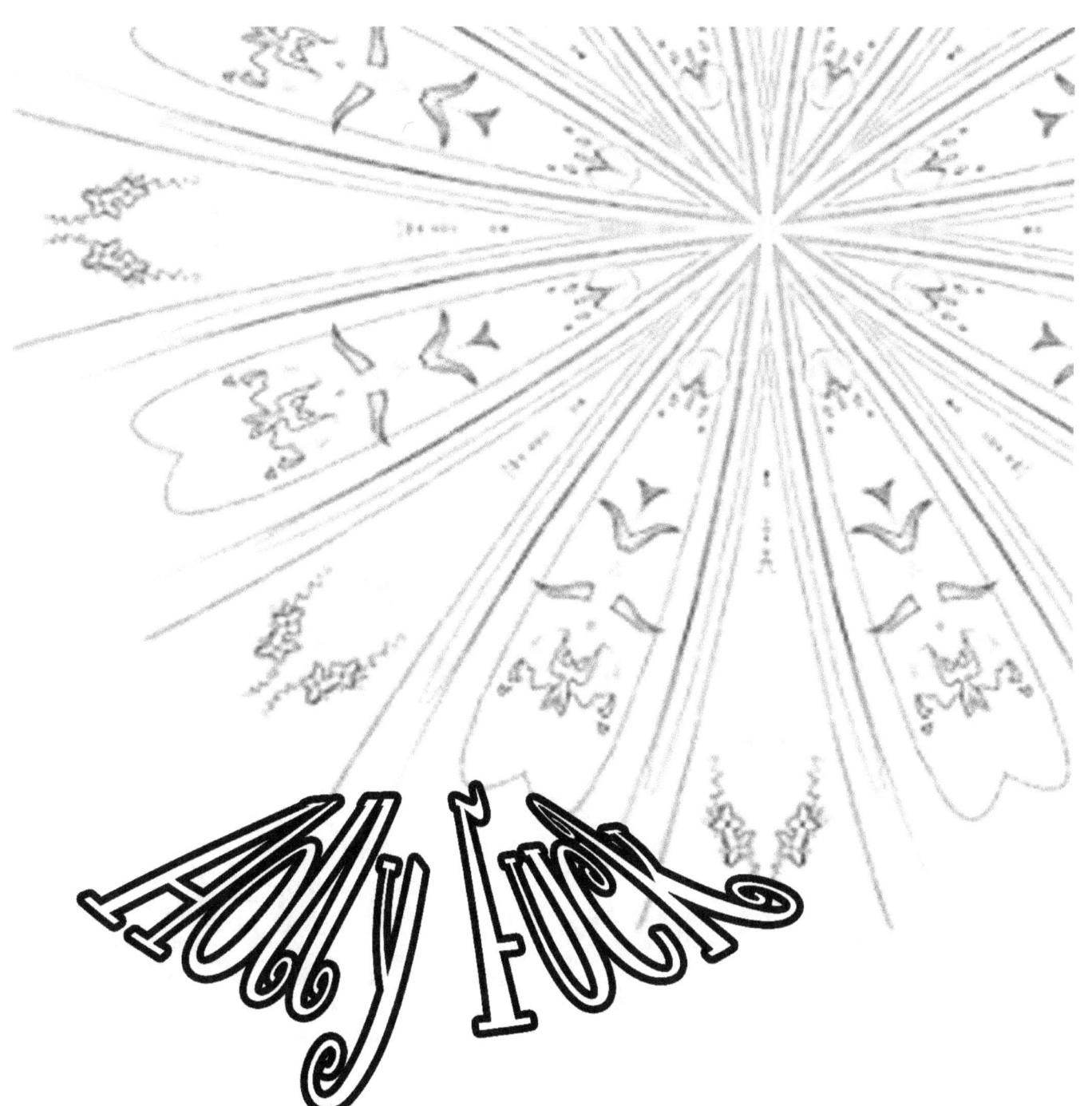

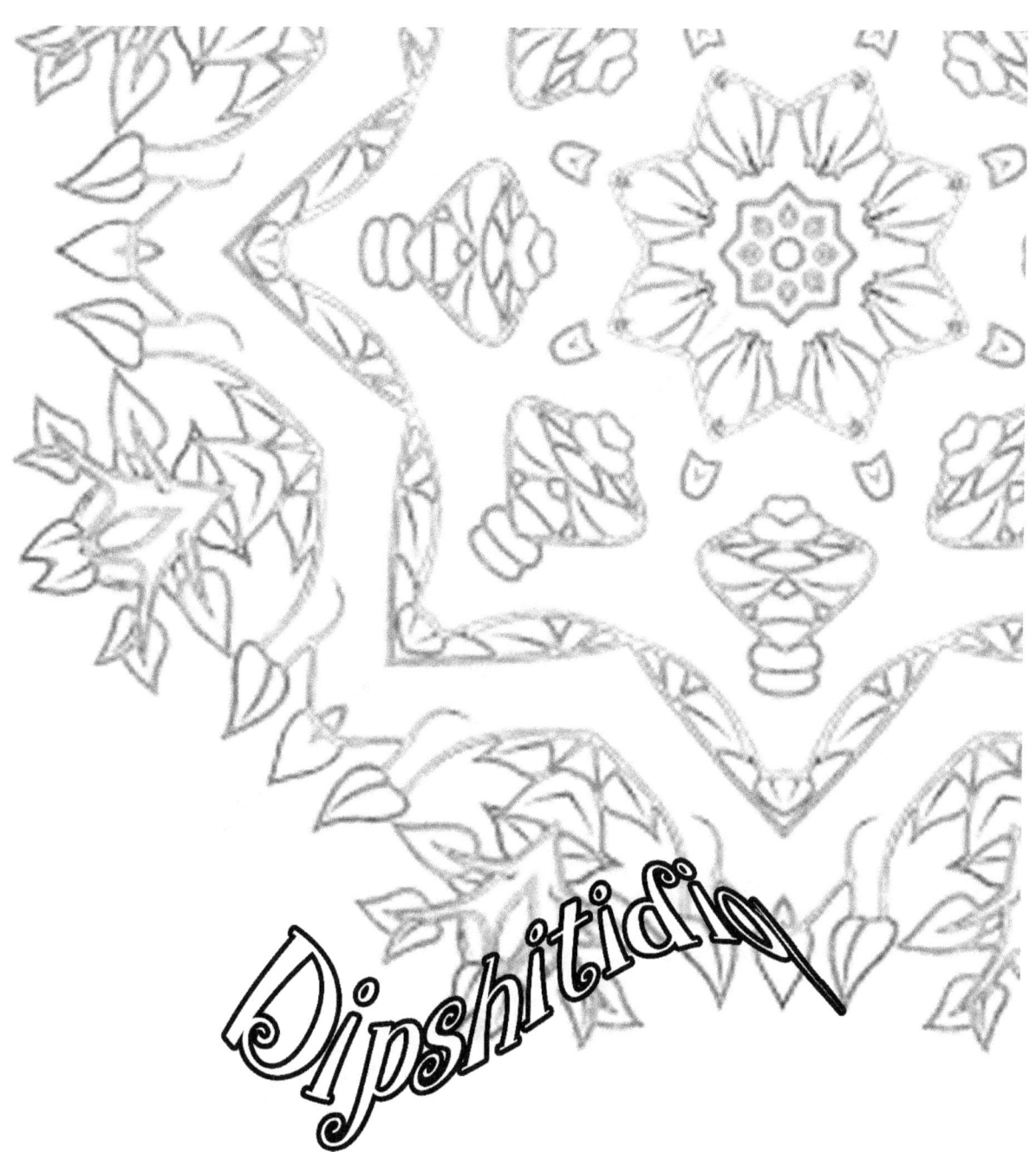

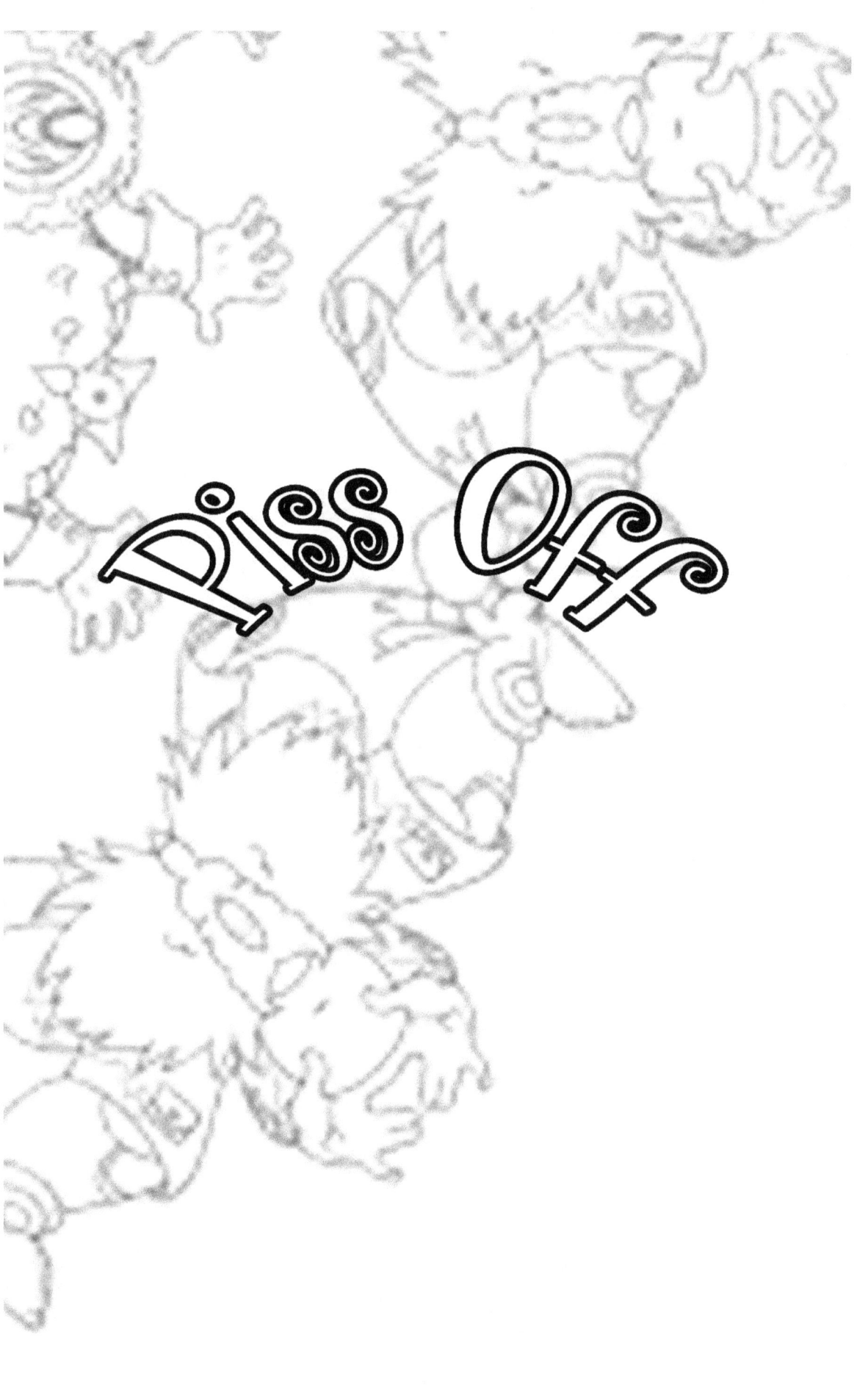

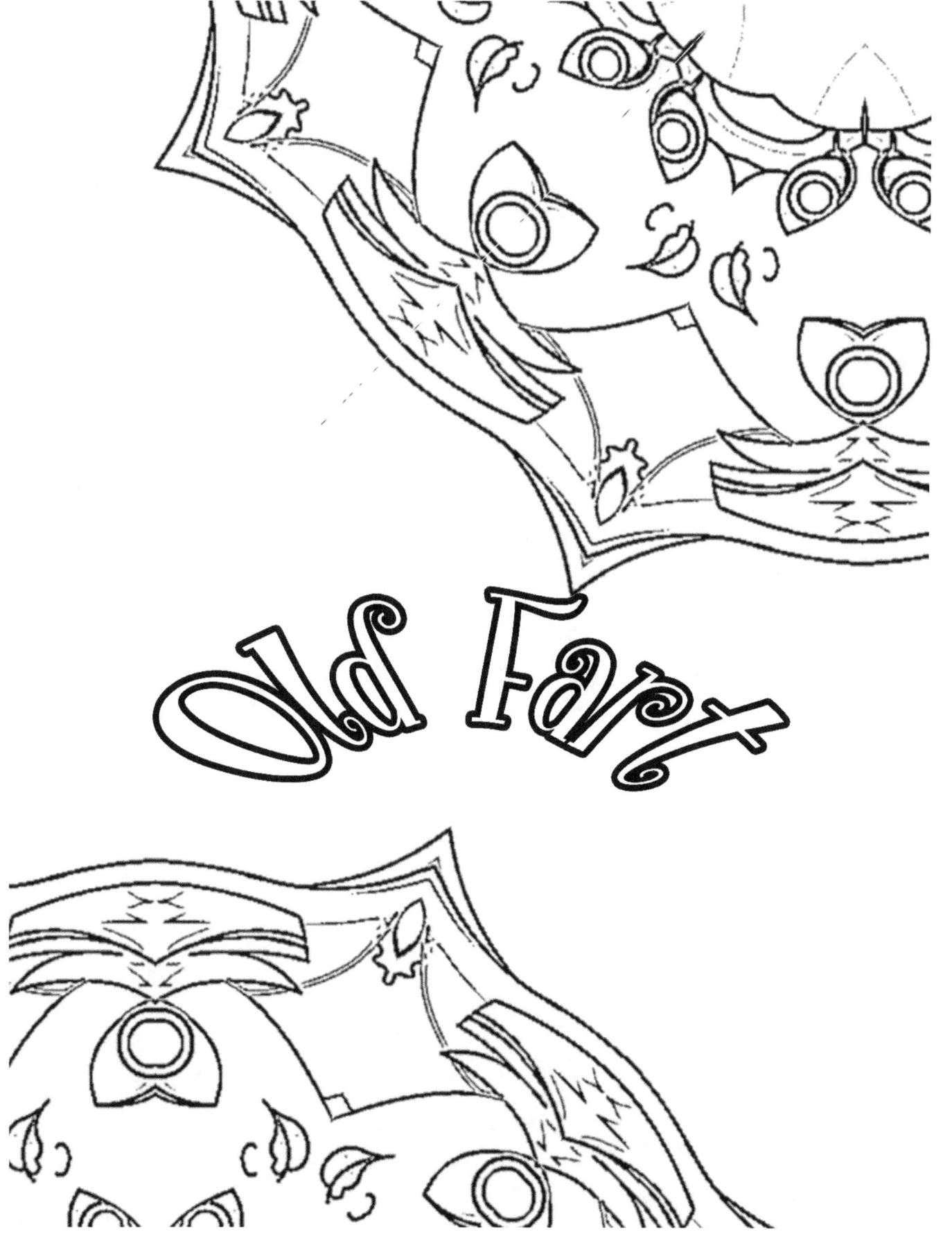

Old Fart

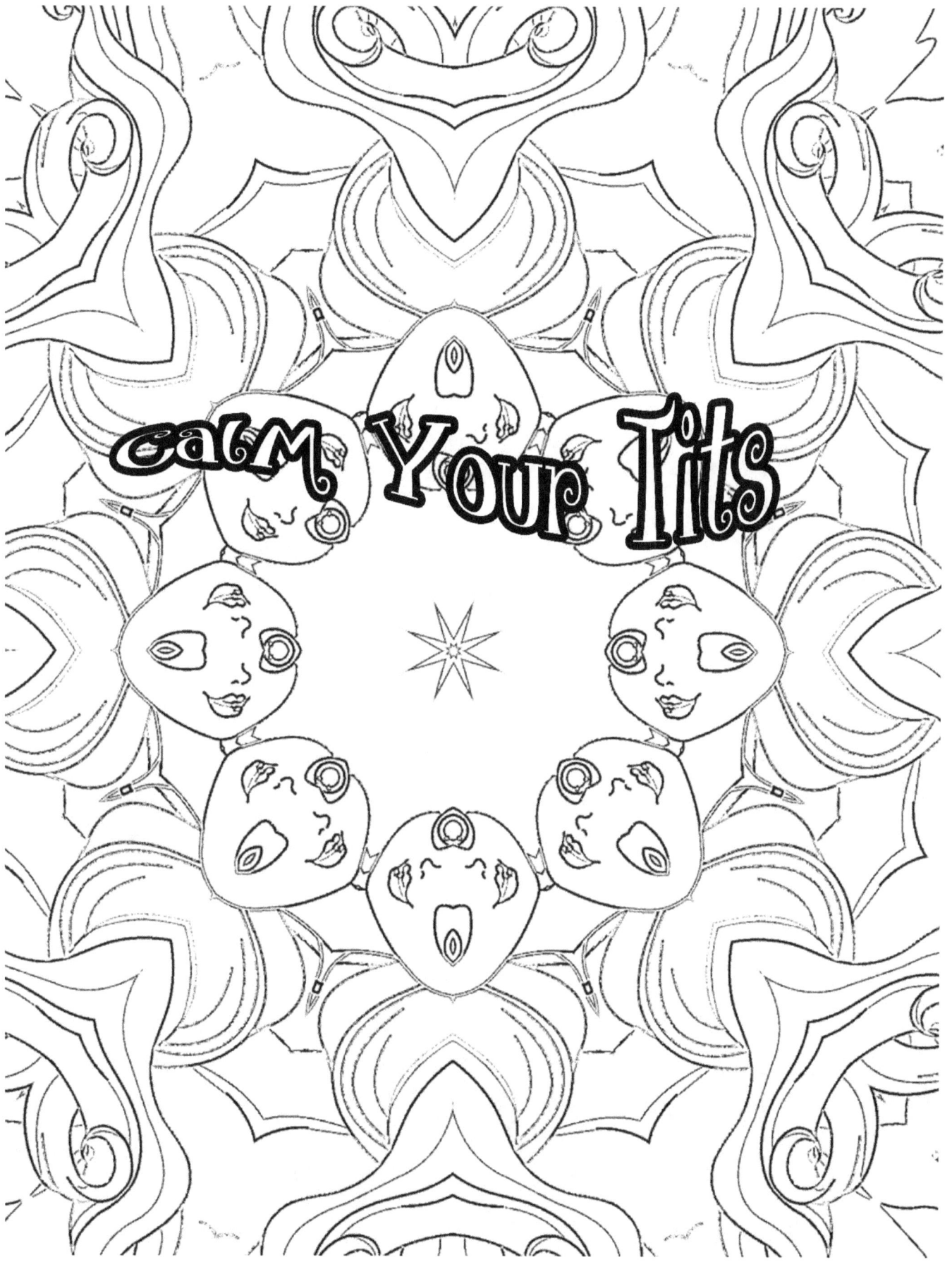

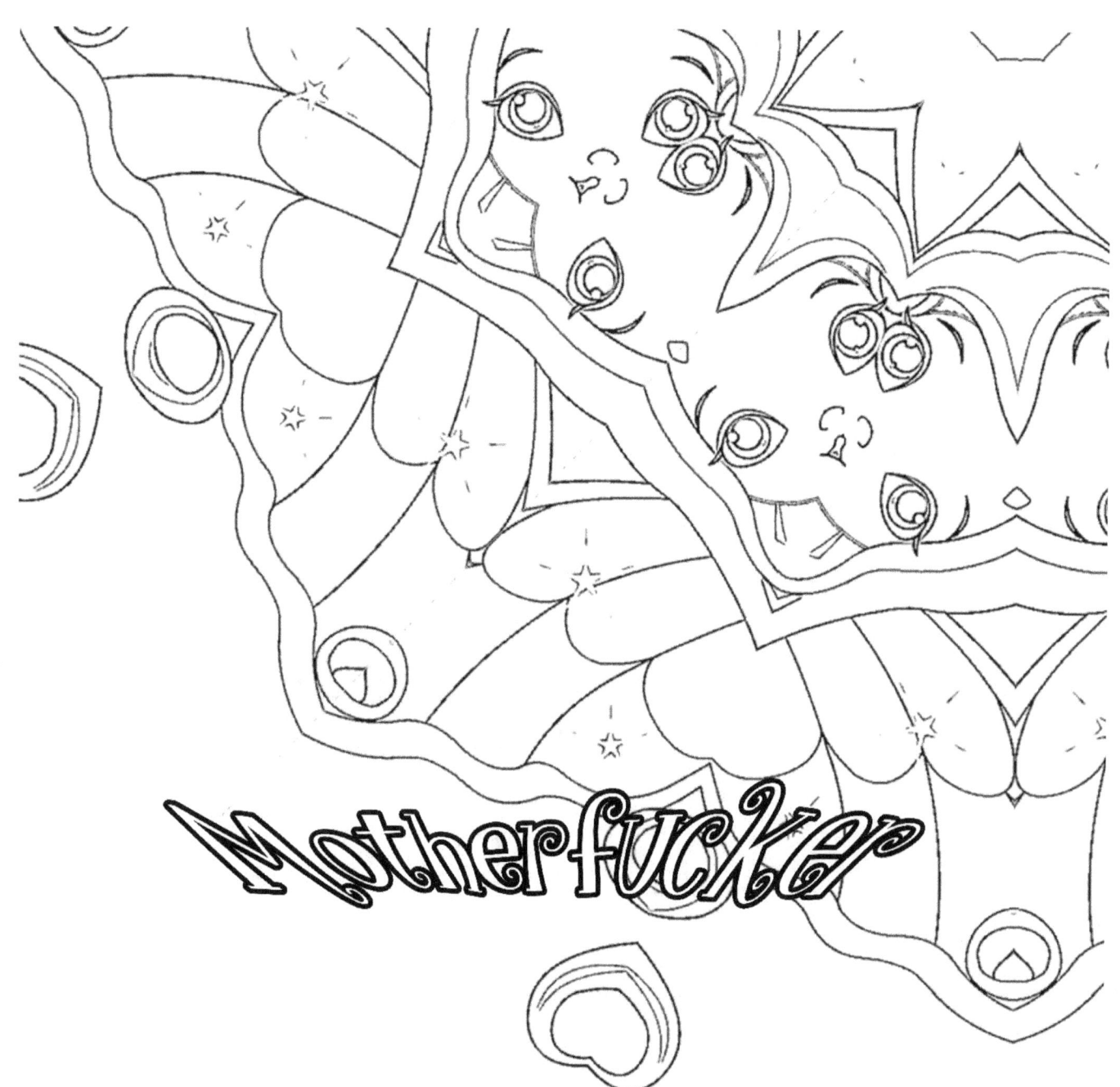

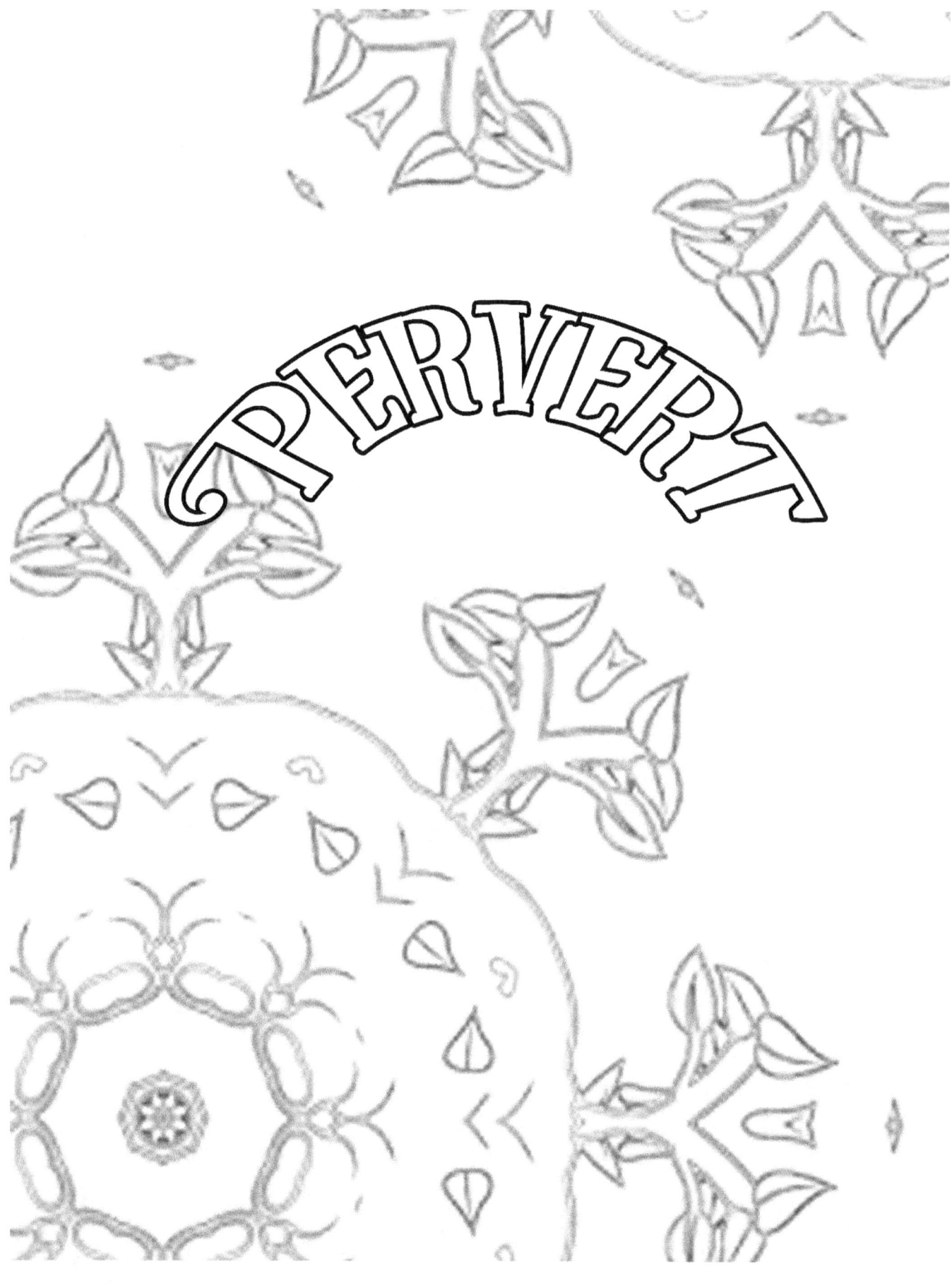

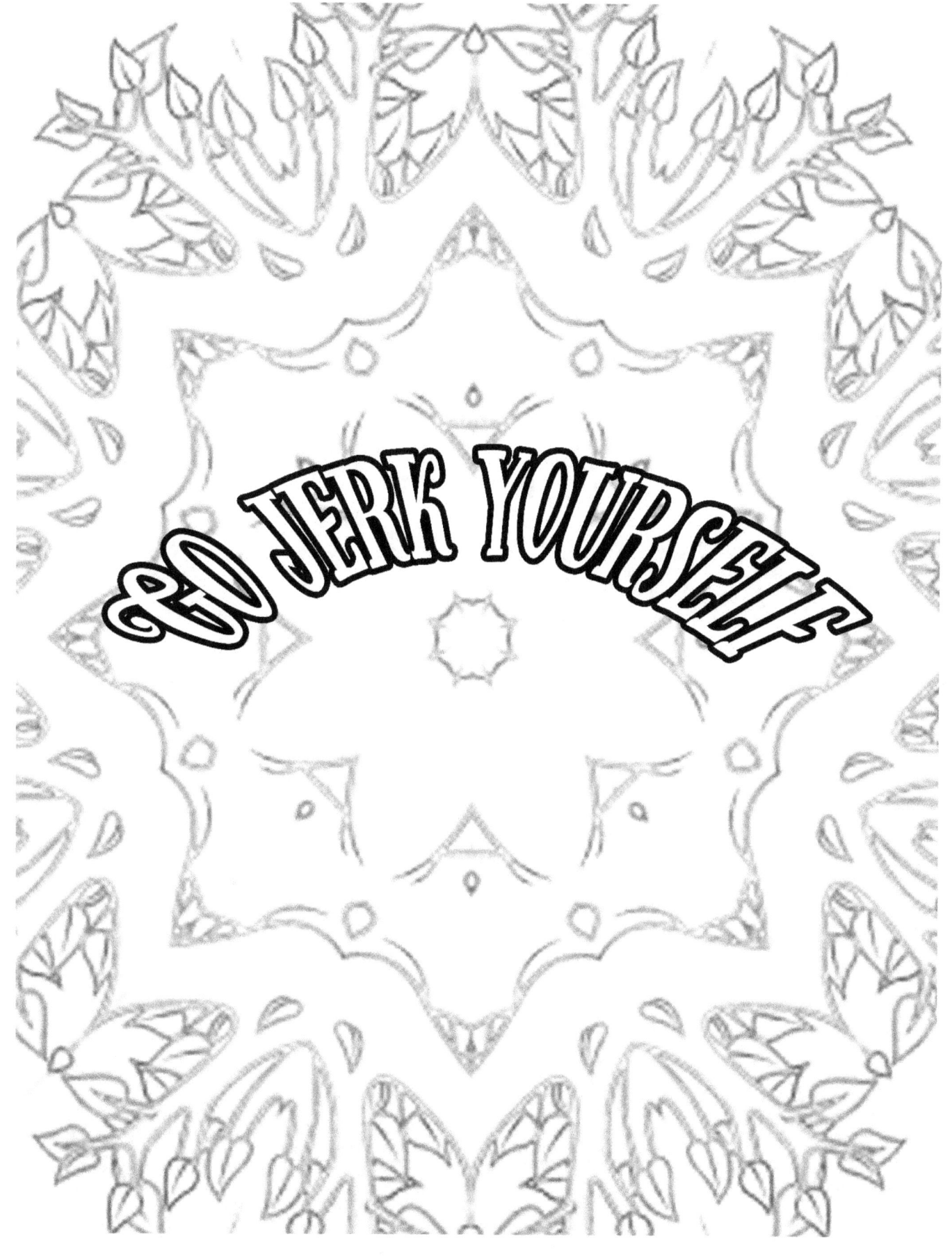

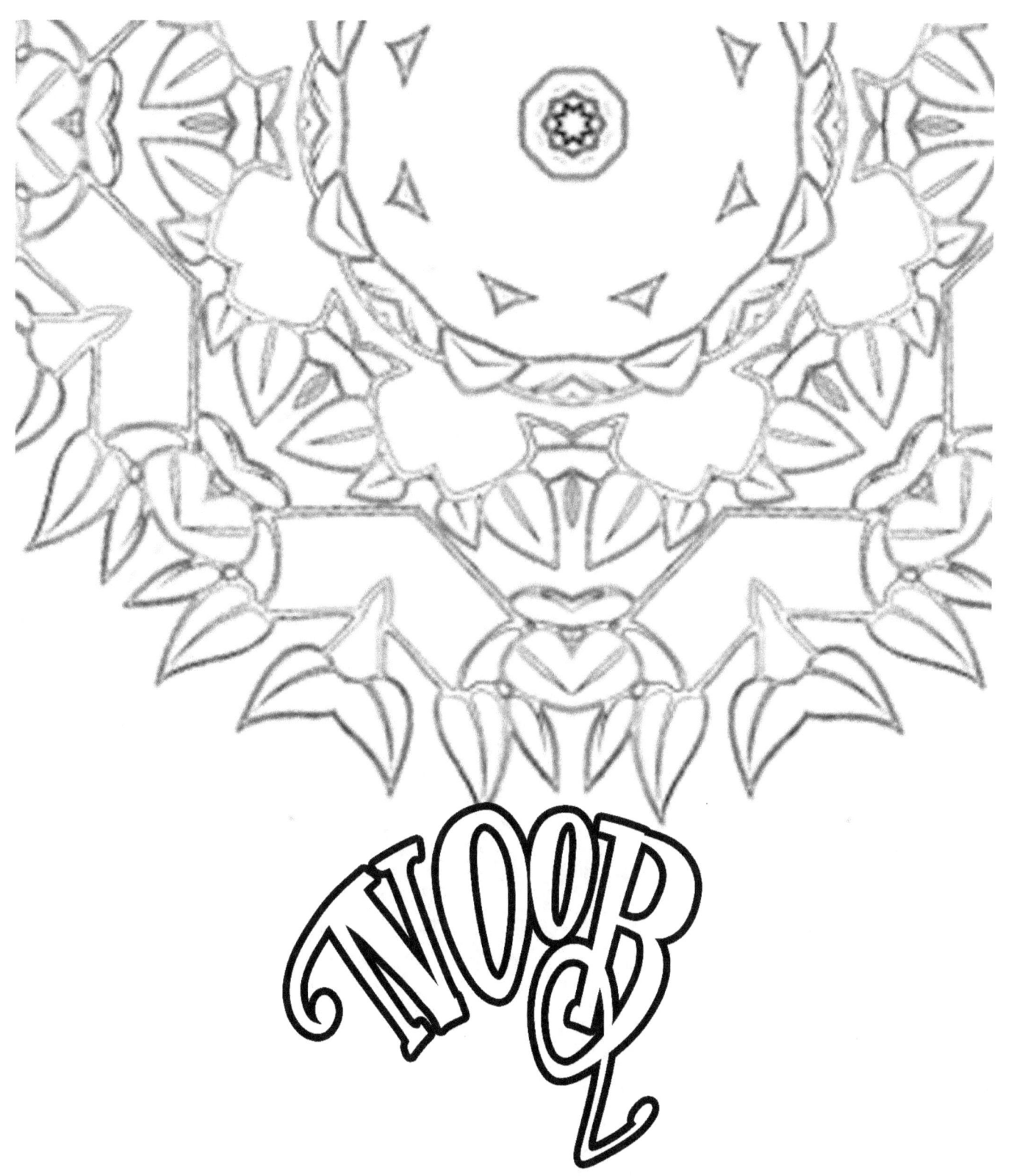

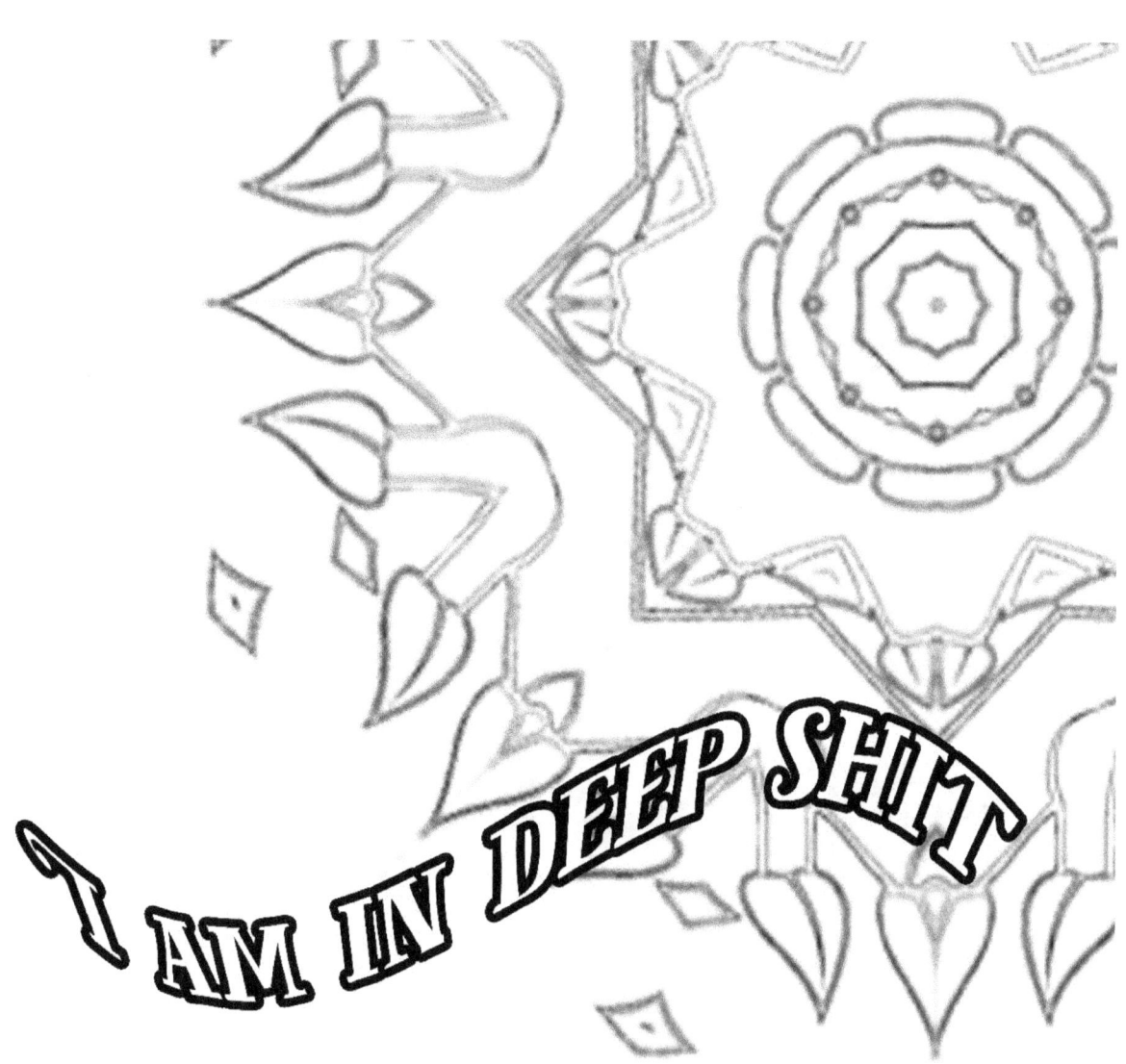

I AM IN DEEP SHIT

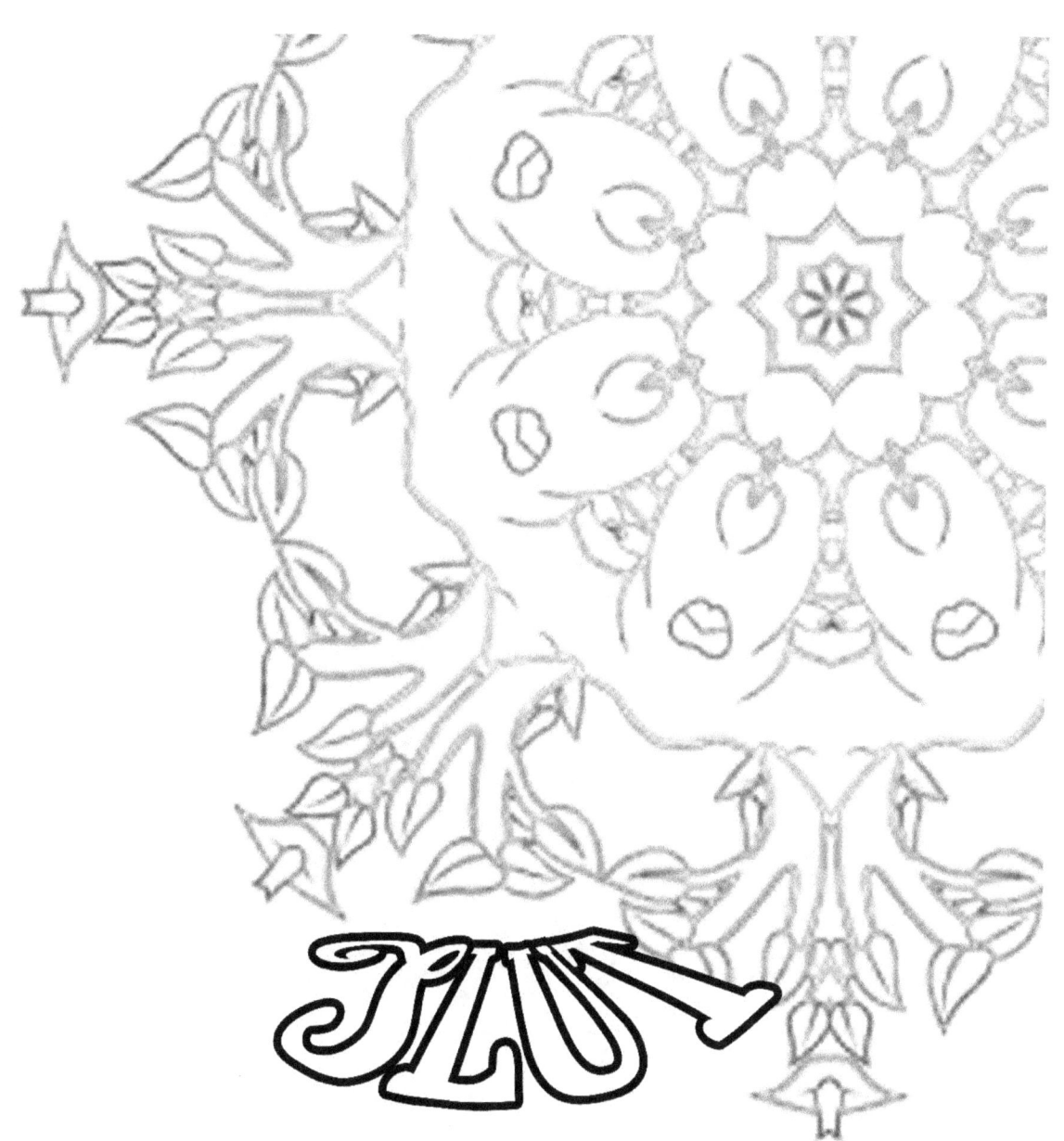

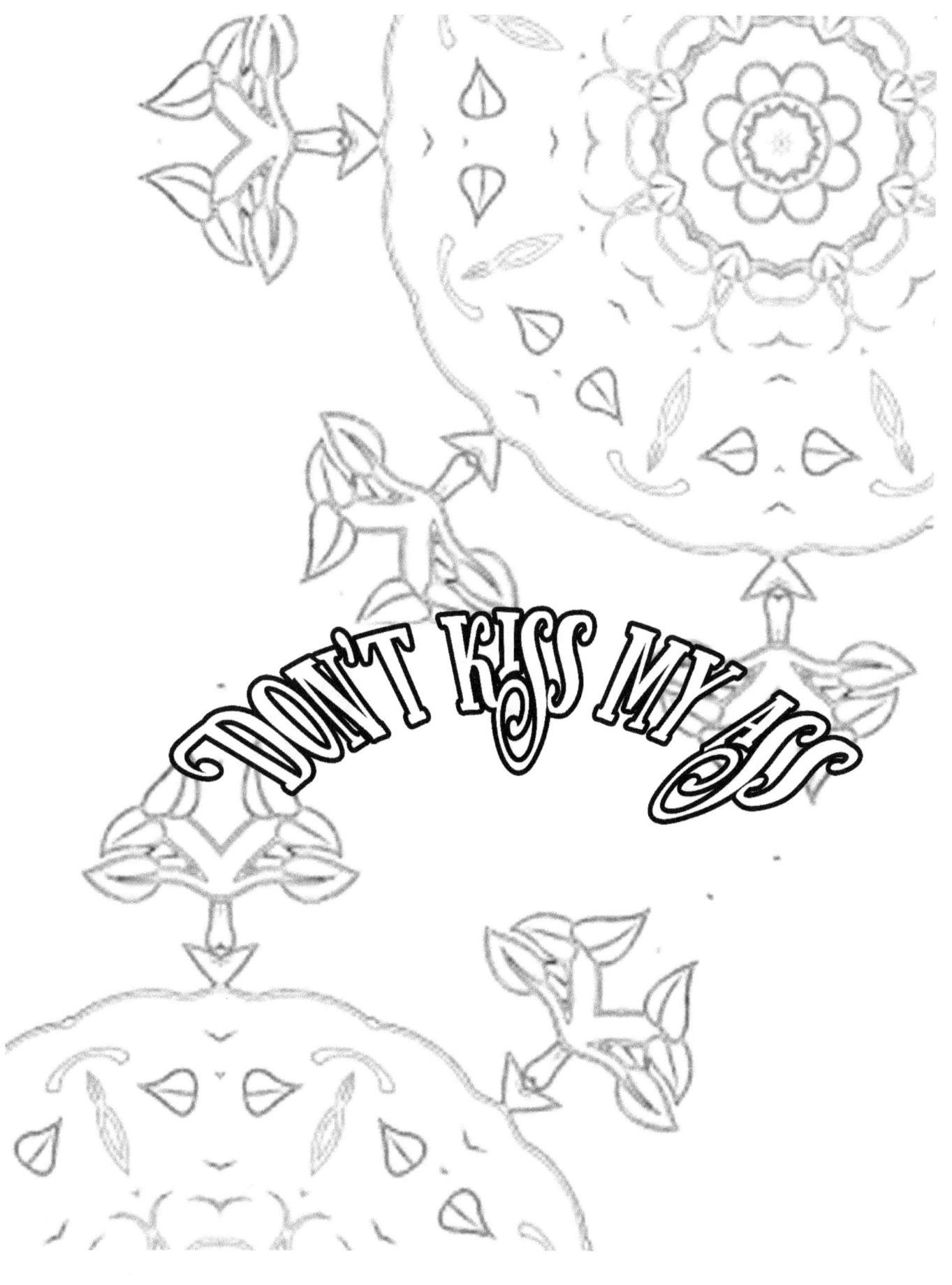

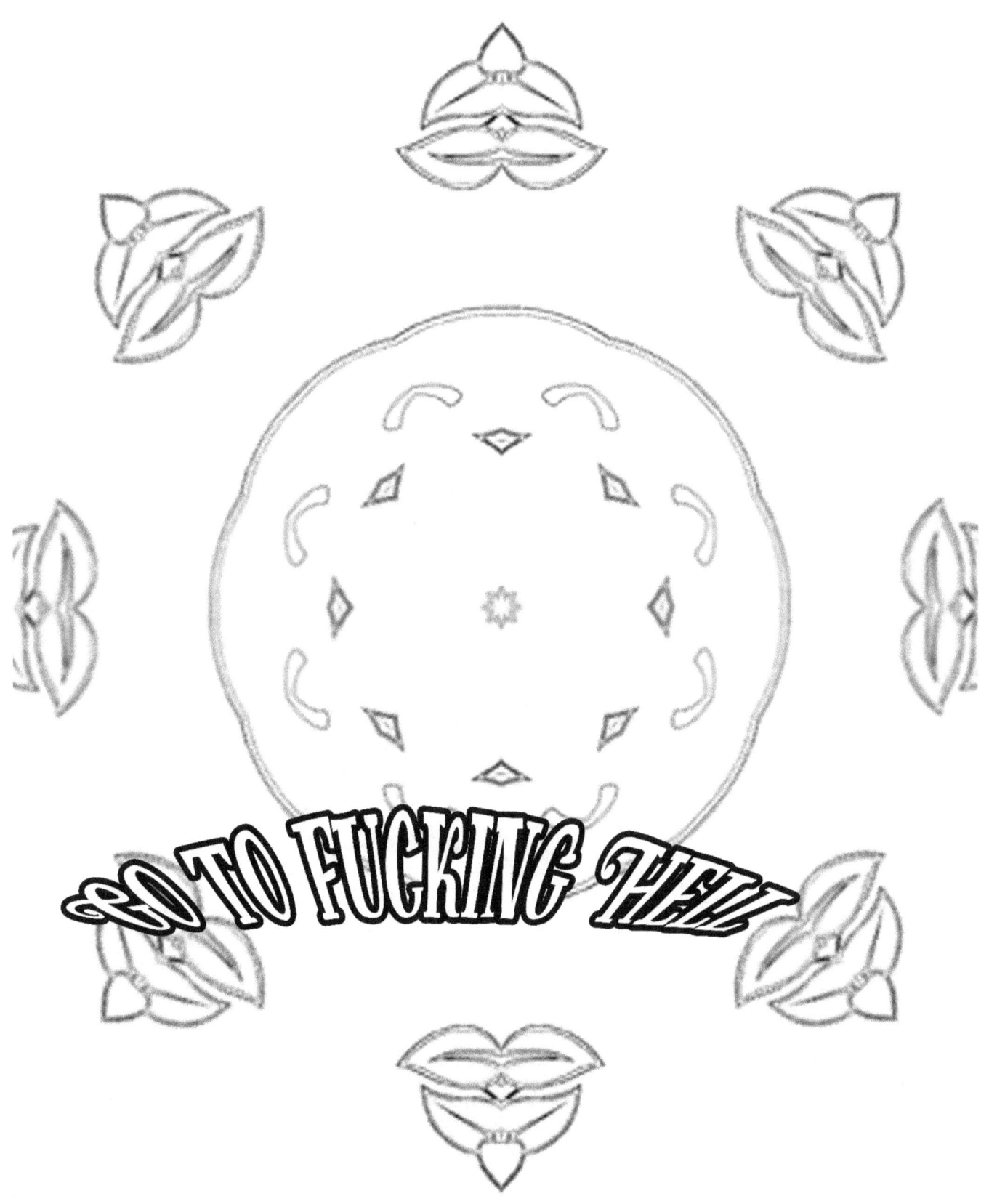

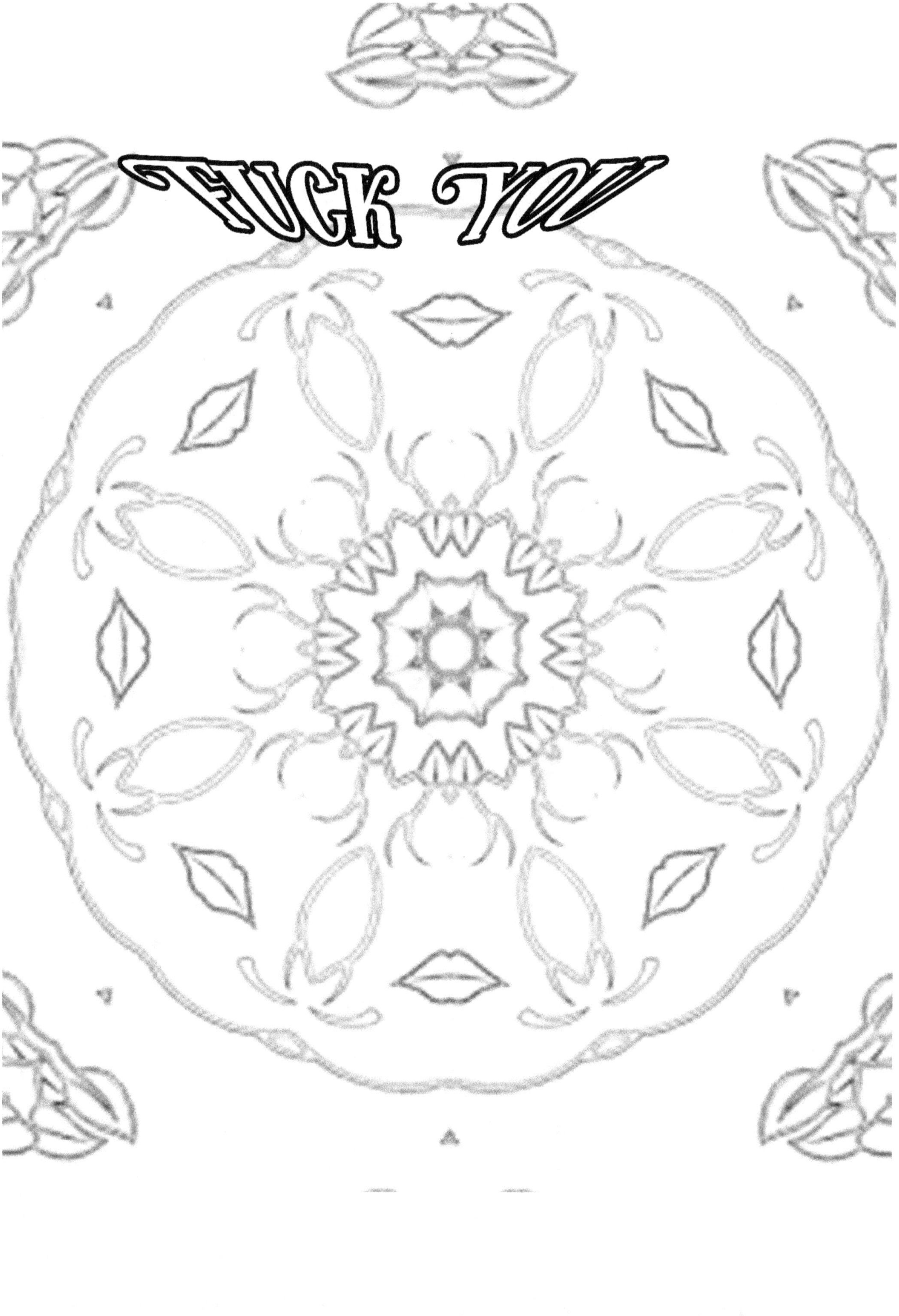

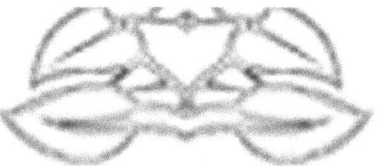

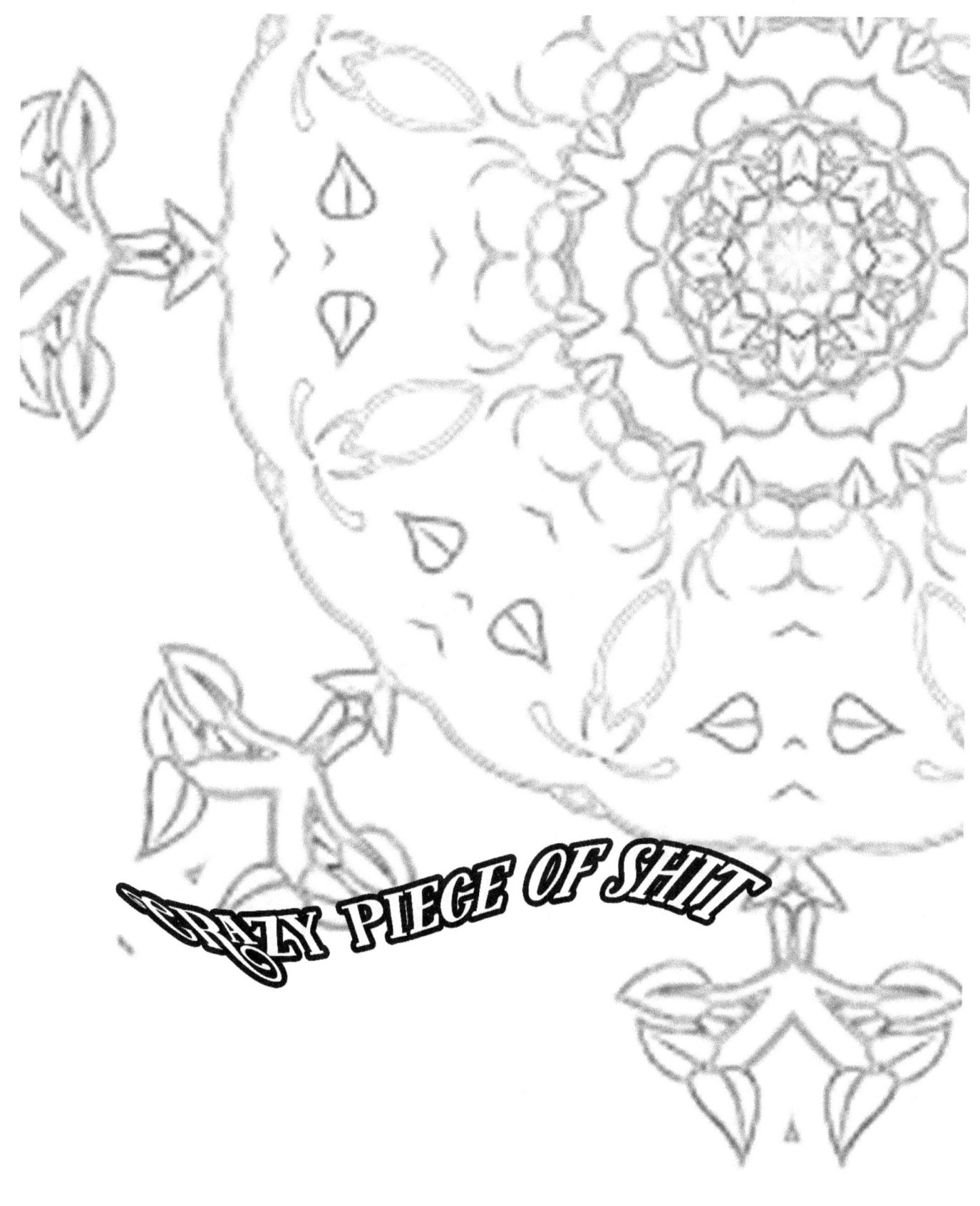

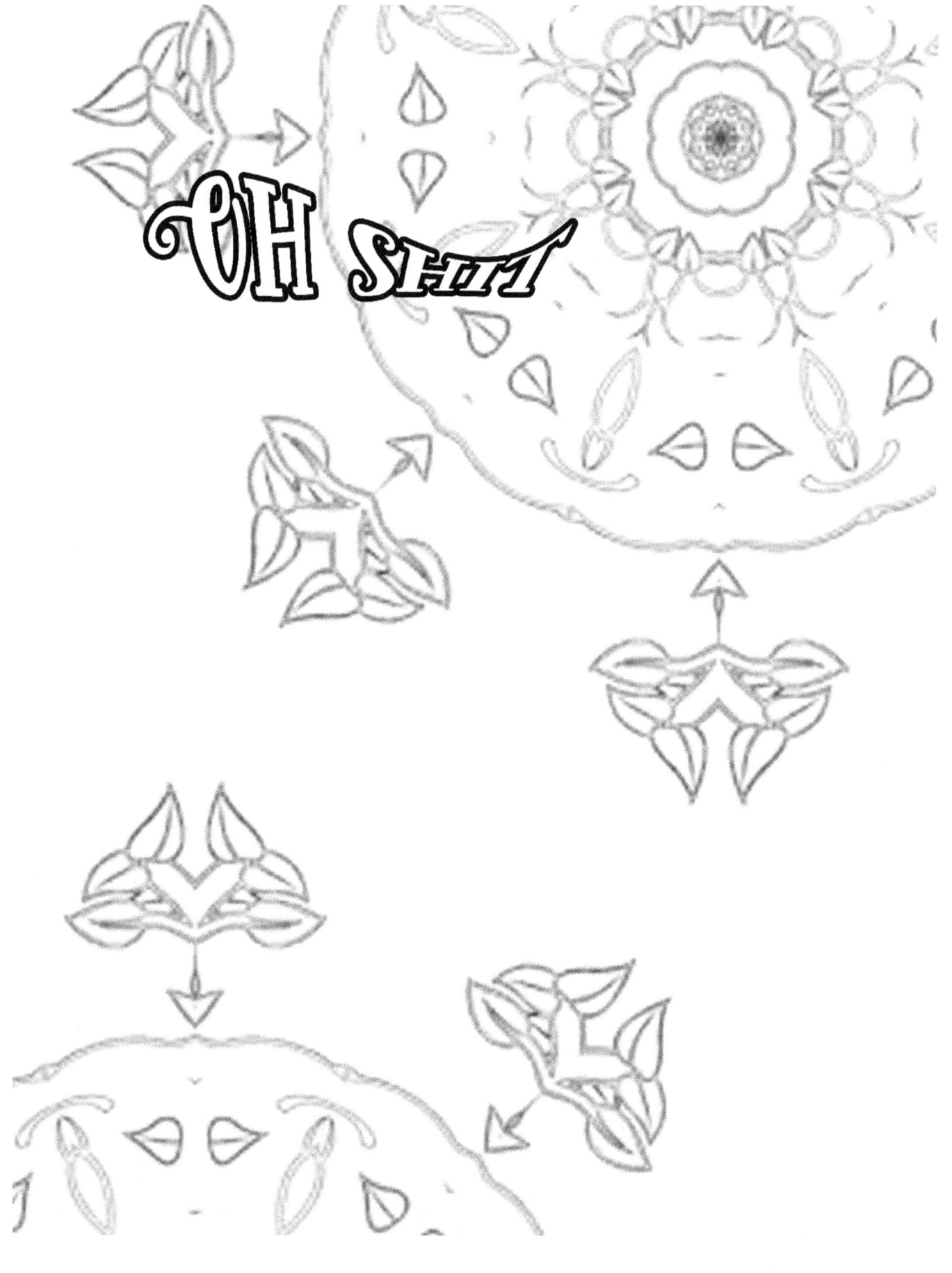

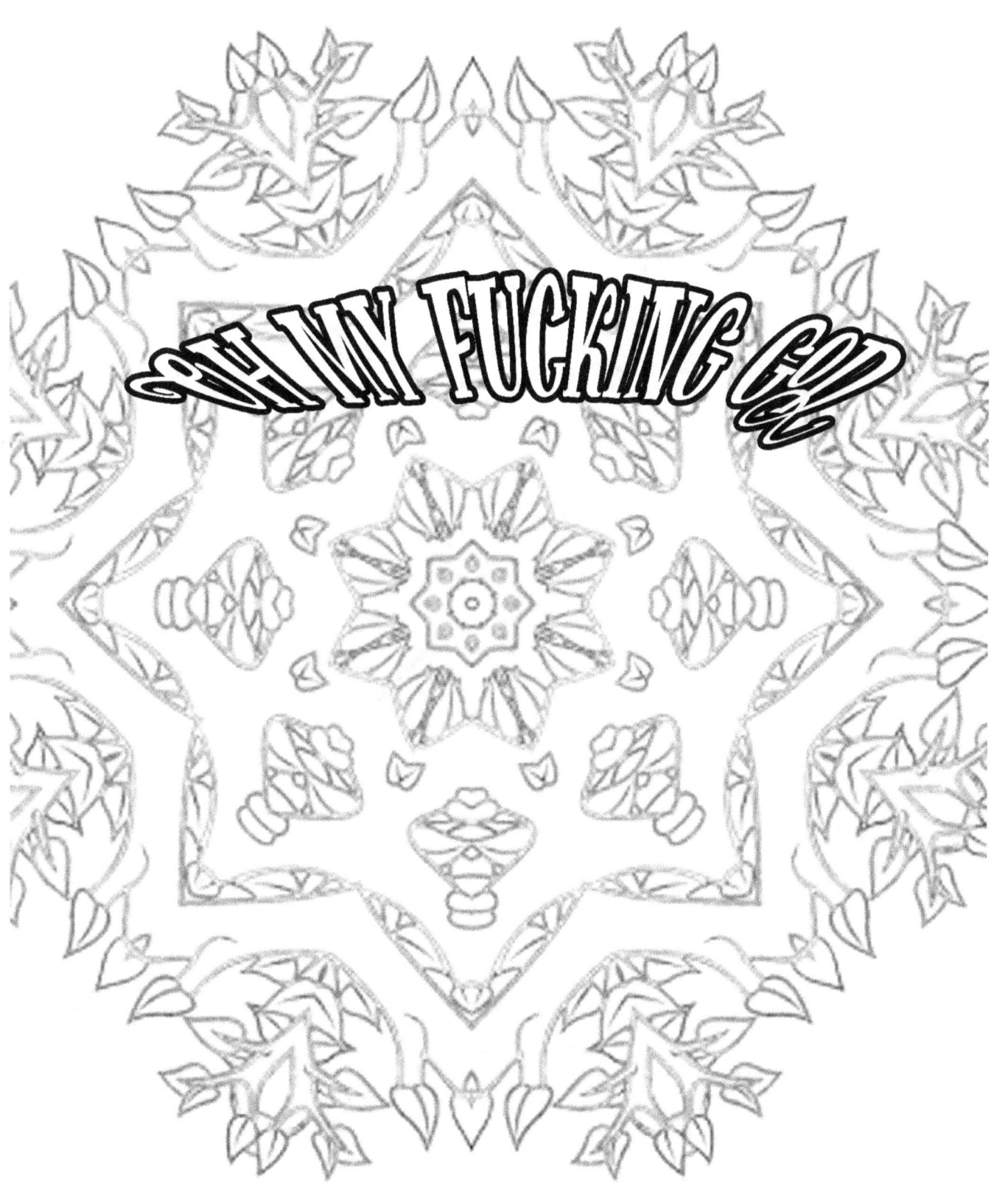

GET THE FUCK OUT

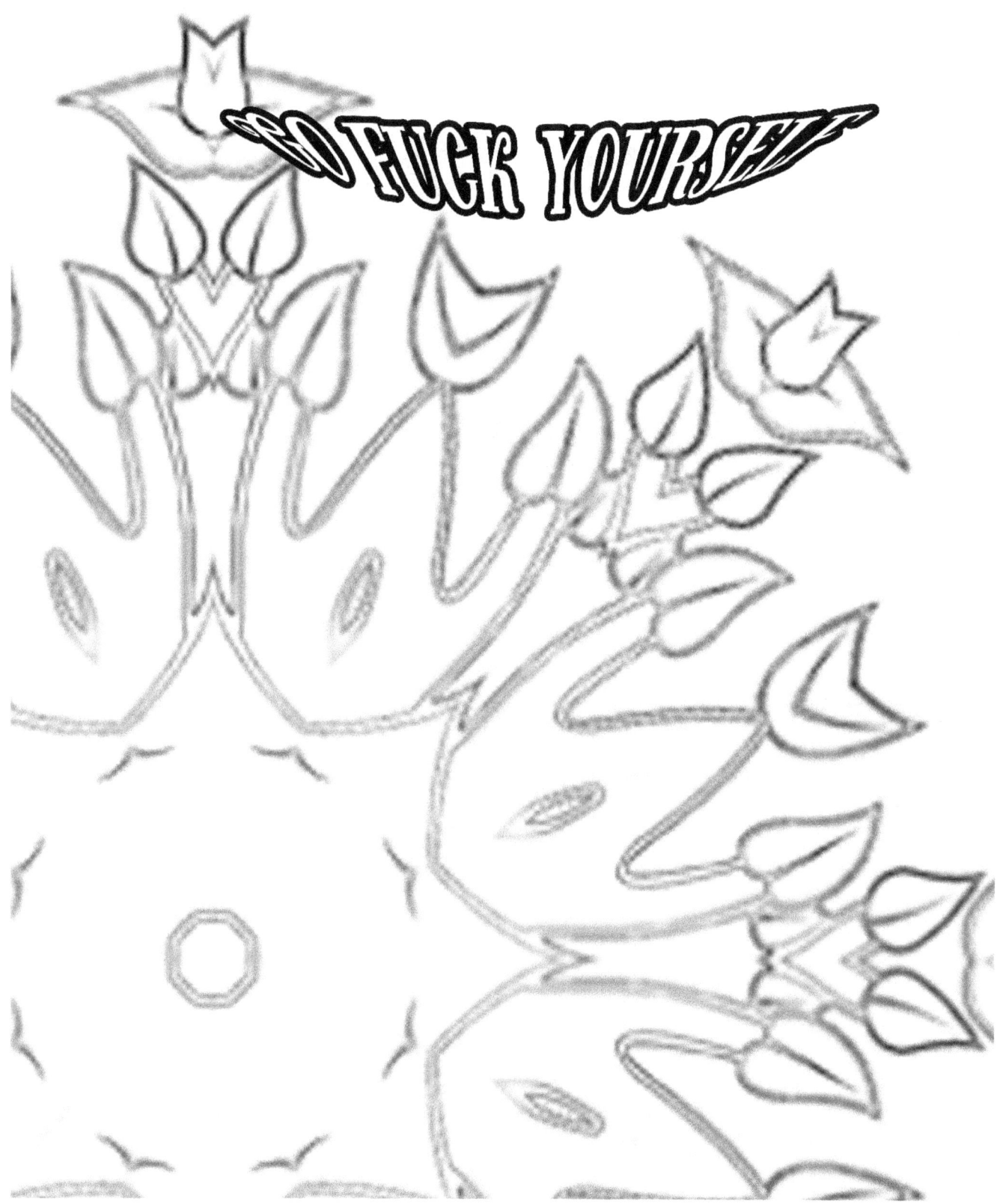

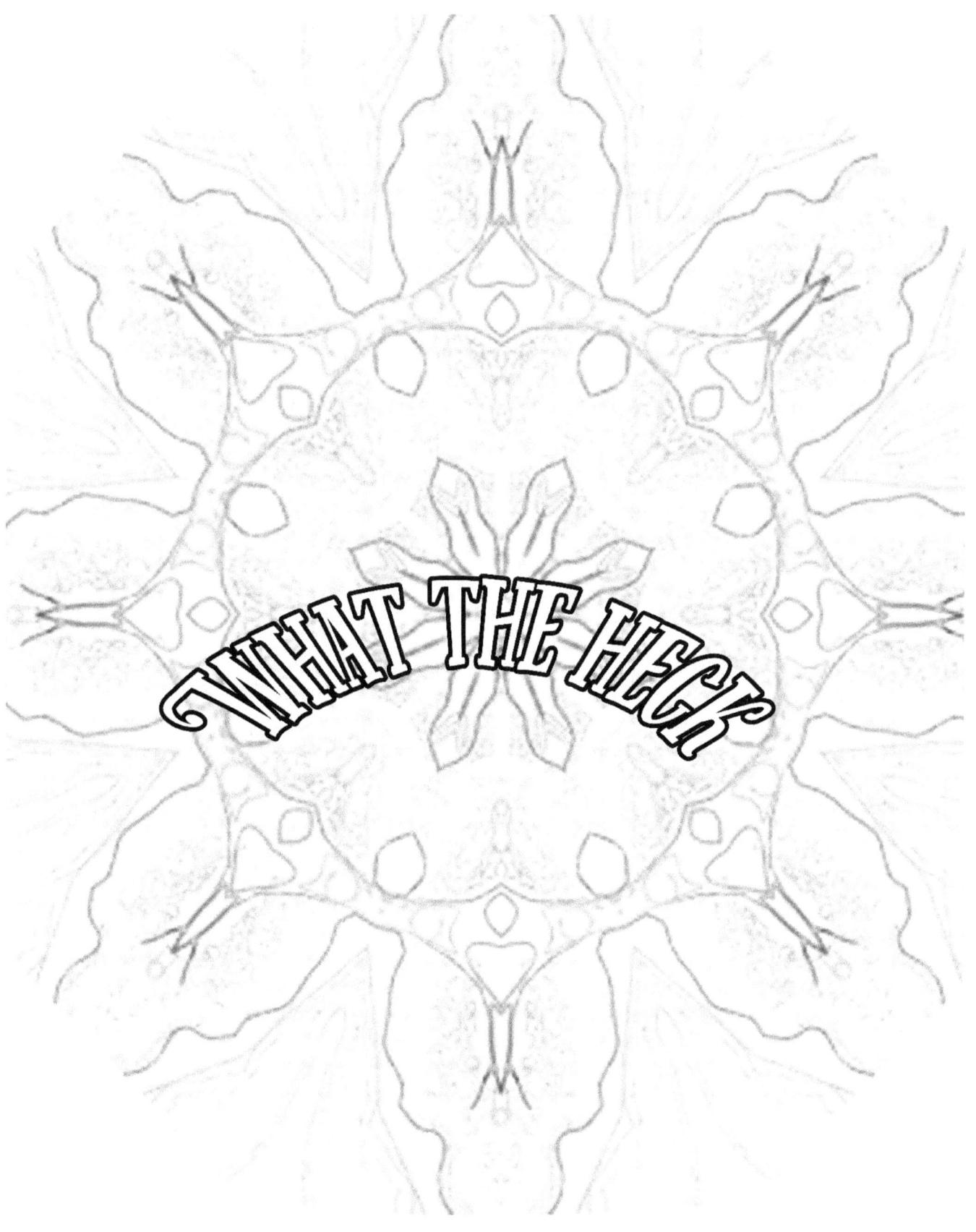

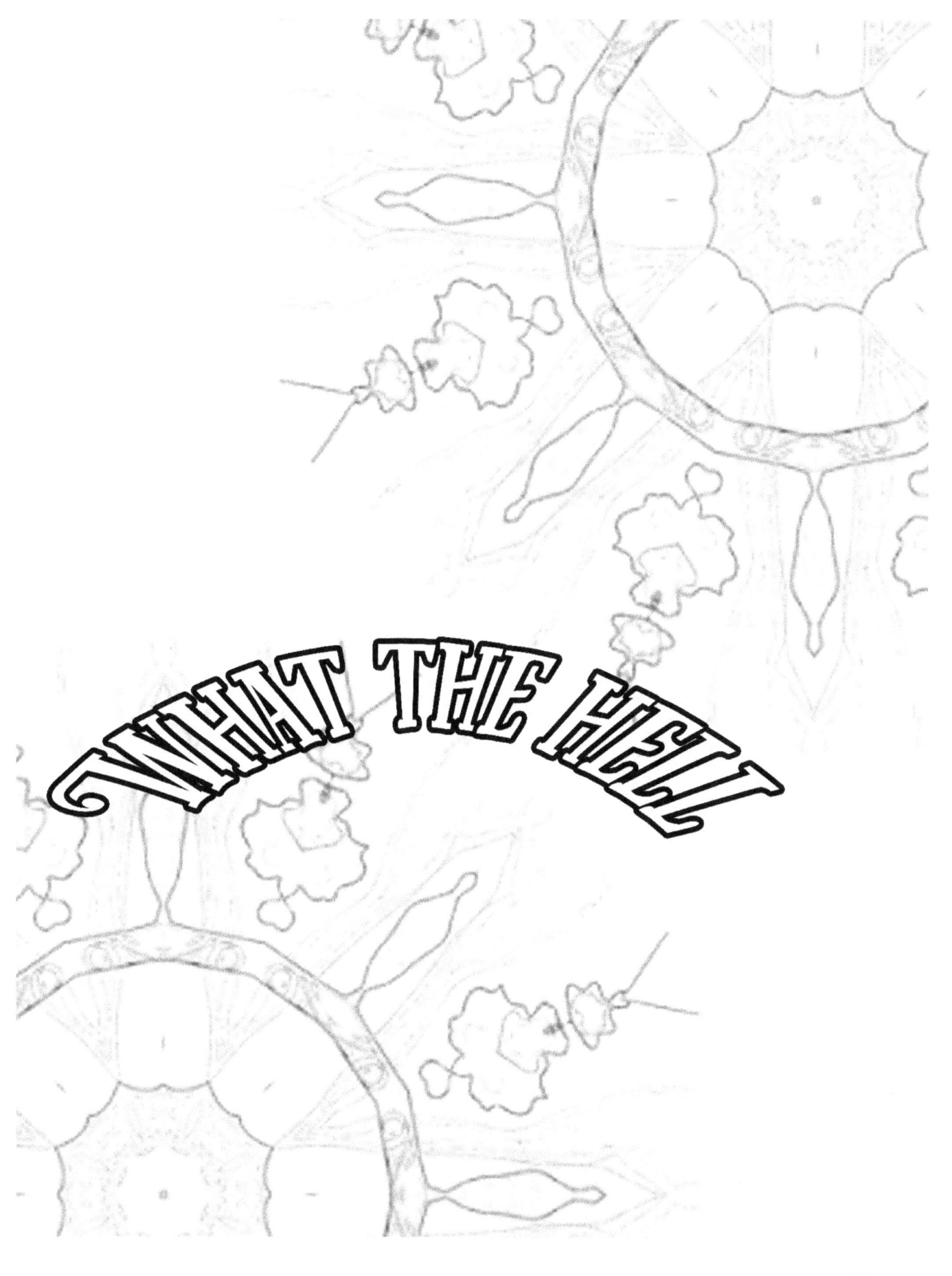